LOVE AND COMPASSION IS MY RELIGION

LOVE AND COMPASSION IS MY RELIGION

A Beginner's Book into Spirituality

Jane Zarse

© 2016 Jane Zarse
All rights reserved.

ISBN: 151695095X
ISBN 13: 9781516950959
Library of Congress Control Number: 2015913680
CreateSpace Independent Publishing Platform
North Charleston, South Carolina

To my all-loving, all-inclusive God

I am a divorcée who found the love of God through the eyes and soul of a gay man. The love of God has no need for religious exclusions. I was sick, broken, powerless, hopeless, and helpless. I didn't love myself and, because of my distorted ego, didn't even know it. I always believed in God, but I was convinced that God didn't believe in me because of all of my failures and mistakes. When you feel this lost, life becomes very dark, and it is impossible to see any way out. I remained focused on what a disaster I had made out of my life and couldn't see past my horrible circumstances. Focusing on my failures kept me stuck and fueled my feelings of being worthless and unlovable.

Learning that God loved me despite all of my bad decisions gave me hope, and the power of hope saved my life. Knowing that God loves me, flaws and all, gave me a sense of self-worth. Reclaiming my self-worth, self-respect, integrity, and dignity has been the greatest, most loving gift. People need to learn how much God loves them before they can be willing to better their lives and attitudes. They become willing to give up the wrong things, such as alcohol, drugs, cutting, anger, resentments, gambling, codependency, food, or sex addiction. I know for a fact that any of these self-destructive, self-defeating behaviors can be positively treated with the love of God. I have lived this amazing grace firsthand.

Religion with exclusions and judgment had turned me off to God. I view religion as very divisive, though we are all one. I erroneously associated God with judgment and punishment, which added insult to injury for a screw-up like me. I give the church a lot of credit. It does show love, but love is too big for just the church. The church needs love, but love does not need the church. God loves you, is available to you, and wants to help you right now. All you need to do is believe. Belief is the only metric that really matters. I believe the love of God can change, heal, and renew anyone's mind, body, and spirit. I'm real sure because it happened to me. This is my story.

1

"Most men lead lives of quiet desperation and go to the grave with the song still in them."

—Henry David Thoreau

My name is Jane Michele Zarse. I was born in Lake Forest, Illinois, on July 28, 1971. Lake Forest, located thirty miles north of Chicago, is rich in history and natural beauty. As far as childhoods go, the first five years of my life were very uneventful. My family lived in a three-bedroom house in west Lake Buff with a big backyard fully equipped with a swing set. My father was a chemical engineer for Procter & Gamble, and my mother was a stay-at-home mom for me and my brother, Jeff, three and a half years my senior. I don't remember much of this time frame, except that the television was my constant babysitter, and I was substantially raised by PBS.

My parents were both slobs, so we hardly had anybody over. On the rare occasion we were expecting company, this mandated major cleaning up. It was amply clear to me from a very early age that what other people thought of us was a big deal in my house. My mother's maiden name was Madigan, and her family tree had umpteen lines of lineage that came over on the *Mayflower*. Her mother's maiden name was Veach and had just as many lines of lineage—maybe more—also on the *Mayflower*. In fact, my maternal grandmother's sister ran the DAR (Daughters of the American Revolution) Midwestern chapter for years. My great-great-great-grandfather was chief of police of Dublin, Ireland, and my maternal grandfather's first cousin was secretary of agriculture under the first President Bush. Appearances were everything to my mother, and my father was a good provider, so maintaining appearances didn't require too much exaggerating, but omissions were acceptable.

When I was in kindergarten, we moved to a French Normandy Tudor-style home overlooking Lake Michigan in eastern Lake Bluff. The architects of our new home were John Howells and Raymond Hood, the same architects who designed the Tribune Tower. Chicago's Tribune Tower is the product of the most famous architecture competition of the twentieth century. Howells and Hood won first prize of $50,000 for the thirty-six-story, soaring Gothic skyscraper on North Michigan Avenue, completed in 1925. Fragments from more than 120 structures, including the Great Wall of China, are embedded in the iconic tower that was designed to be "the most beautiful office building in the world." No American newspaper is more closely associated with the building that houses it than the *Chicago Tribune*.

Our property was surrounded by mature trees and beautiful lake views, You can see the outline of our slate roof in the opening shot of Robert Redford's *Ordinary People*. In Chicagoland, on the north shore, my mother was utterly convinced that there was a direct correlation between proximity to Lake Michigan and certain social expectations. Our house was on the lake, and it was very clear that I needed to look and act the part. I went from wearing smock dresses from Kmart to Izod, Lilly Pulitzer, and Florence Eiseman. This is what the popular girls were wearing, so my mother thought mimicking their style would help me fit in—and it did. Kids were commonly mocked for not donning the designer brands, and I was relieved that I wasn't ridiculed for my clothing.

Our next-door neighbors were the Tutwiler family, and they had the old-money, country-club style that impressed the hell out of my mother. Mr. Tutwiler (Tut, as we affectionately called him) grew up in a family-owned hotel and was accustomed to being waited on. He also owned a paper company and a seat on the Options Exchange. His wife, Leslie, was very classy, kind, and generous. She was the kind of woman who would give you the shirt off her back. She was an excellent hostess and was always offering up food and drinks, but she never drank a drop of alcohol in all the decades we knew her. You could tell she could recognize the north shore bullshit for what it was and didn't buy into it. They had two older children who were out East at boarding school, and their daughter, Annie, was a year older than me and attended a private day school in Lake Forest. They all had their own county club. Tut frequented Exmoor in Highland Park, Leslie had the Bath and Tennis Club in Lake Bluff, and Annie had the Winter Club in Lake Forest. They also had a winter house in Naples, Florida. Naples was commonly referred to as "little Lake Forest" in the '80s.

Across the street resided the Bryants. Mr. Bryant was a Brown graduate and had countless, impressive patents with Abbott Laboratories. His wife, Julie, was extremely bright and talented in her own right, but she was constantly struggling with alcoholism, which robbed her of her potential. She had a sharp, dry wit and could really make my mom howl with laughter. They had two daughters: Lori, a year older than me, and Katie, two years my junior. Like me, both girls also attended Lake Bluff East School.

I grew up in much more carefree days. I would ride my bike to and from school, and parents would let us go out and play unattended until bedtime. The new house came with built-in playmates for me, which was terrific. I have warm memories of playing kick the can until it got dark, sledding down the bluff in the winter, and enjoying the beach in the summer. I could ride my bike into town, and my family had a charge account at Lake Bluff Pharmacy. I could charge whatever I wanted. I don't recall ever being scolded for abusing this privilege, even though I chronically charged unnecessary items. No cash required.

My father is of German descent and has always had an unbelievable work ethic. My parents met at the University of Wisconsin, and my mother says one of the reasons she married my father is because she was certain success was in his future. My dad was still working at Procter & Gamble during the day, but he started also working at Plantation Bakery at night. This was a huge family secret at the time. Retrospectively, I find this covert omission ridiculous. My best guess is we didn't want people to think that my dad's nine-to-five gig didn't cut it. That "shameful" secondary income allowed my parents to start gobbling up single-family homes in Chicago suburbs, such as Mundelein and Buffalo Grove, and they started fixing them up and renting them out. A large part of my elementary school weekends were spent in home repair stores. I spent hours upon hours in the appliance or the carpet sections. I even met Bob Vila. My brother, Jeff, invariably opted to stay home.

Jeff was four school grades ahead of me, so we rarely had any friends or activities in common. I followed him in both the Lake Bluff public school system and in the private Lake Forest Academy for high school. He was a hard act to follow. He placed first in the state of Illinois in a math competition. When he was in junior high, he was taking high-school classes in Zion, and when he was at the Academy, he was also attending Lake Forest College. Every Ivy League college he applied to accepted him, and he early decisioned Dartmouth. Prospective teacher after teacher, expecting another genius, couldn't help but be disappointed in me. I could see it on their faces. Each seemed more disappointed than the last.

My dad has always been adept with anything electrical and mechanical. Being a landlord to all of these rental properties really honed his skills. Like a lot of people in our new neighborhood, the Tutwilers had help. Bertha and Wardel were a lovely couple. Bertha would clean, and Wardel would help around the house a few days a week. Bertha ultimately ended up working for my mother, too, and felt like a member of our family. As my mother developed a friendship with Leslie, my dad would take care of handyman duties when Wardel wasn't around. Tut's Options Exchange seat fascinated both my parents, and the concept of trading was very appealing but also seemed risky. My mother had vision and stones for my father and her children, but never for herself. She knew she had to build my father up and extend him unwavering support to get behind the trading concept, which she did. The secondary income afforded him the ability to rent a seat on a trial basis. This trial basis was successful, and my father ended up purchasing an Options Exchange seat and eventually became a full member of the Chicago Board of Trade for over twenty-five years.

2

"If you know how to be satisfied, you are rich."

—Lao Tzu

It was very clear that we were wealthy beyond my family's wildest dreams. It was the '80s, and my parents were millionaires. I transferred to Lake Forest Country Day School (LFCDS) for the start of seventh grade. LFCDS, founded in 1888, is a coeducational day school (prekindergarten to grade eight) located on a twenty-nine-acre campus in Lake Forest, Illinois. Modern-day tuition for seventh grade is approximately $25,000. I was now attending school with an old-money class structure that marginally resembled feudalism. Many small fortunes were made the easy way; they started with a large one. As usual, my mother had me prepared. I showed up decked out in designer duds, broadly talented (due to years of training in dance), and pretty. In Lake Forest, there was always a prettier girl than me. Always.

Around this time, my parents decided they wanted a lakefront estate in Lake Forest. A riparian property was a must. My mother always stated that only three things matter with real estate: location, location, location. The ninety-two-hundred-square-foot home sits on 1.8 acres of water views and has two staircases, an elevator, a wall safe, thirteen bathrooms, and a private beach. Our house was designed by James Gamble Rogers, an American architect best known for his academic commissions at Yale University, Columbia University, and Northwestern University. The house came with a live-in gardener we called William. William also worked at the Swift and Donnelley estates but lived with us. We still kept the Lake Bluff house and leased it out as another rental property.

I was quite popular at my new school. In fact, my parents were called into the day school and apprised that my sort of popularity for a new girl was unusual with this crowd. This crowd all grew up together, with parents in the same upper-crust, tight-knit social circle. This didn't faze me. The boys liked me, and the girls included me, too. I was invited to every party.

I took up field hockey like an old pro. My first year playing, I was the number-one scorer on the team. I also won Miss All-Around for the gymnastics competition. I took formal dancing lessons, white gloves and all, at Onwentsia Club. This exclusive country club hosted the US Open in 1906. Most of my classmates' parents belonged to this prestigious club, and the fact that my parents didn't and weren't a part of this inner circle was not lost on me.

It was customary for LFCDS graduates to attend boarding school, typically out East. Many of my classmates went on to Phillips Exeter Academy, the Hotchkiss School, Saint George's School, Deerfield Academy, and Berkshire School. We took PSAT classes. We were prepping for admittance to prep school. In the 1980s, LFCDS went up to ninth grade, and most of us graduated grade nine. In my humble opinion, getting into some of these stellar schools was easier coming from grade nine as opposed to straight out of junior high.

Right before graduation, a nurse visited our gym glass. I was fourteen and had just gotten my period and started wearing a bra. I was a really late bloomer and a strange kid in the sense that I fooled around with boys but secretly still played with dolls. The nurse asked us to bend over and touch our toes. I learned that I had scoliosis, and my mother and I had to go downtown and see a specialist. I was informed that I had to wear a back brace with the neck brace, like the one in *Sixteen Candles*, eighteen hours a day. I was scheduled to go to France the summer of 1986, but our class trip was canceled due to Gaddafi and terrorism. Instead, I spent that summer at home, in our big, beautiful home, trapped in a back brace. The timing couldn't have been better. I grew three and a half inches that summer. I was very careful never to let any of my peers spot me in my brace. When I started Lake Forest Academy in the fall, I only had to sleep in the damn thing at night.

I started sophomore year at the Lake Forest Academy in the fall of 1986. My brother had graduated in 1985 and was attending Dartmouth College in Hanover, New Hampshire. The Academy is a highly selective, prestigious college preparatory boarding and day school founded in 1857. I was a day student, but we literally had students from all over the world. The Academy cultivates appreciation of diversity and multiculturalism. The school is committed to global awareness and understanding. Modern-day tuition is roughly $35,000 for day students and $47,000 to board. My parents also made financial donations annually while I was in attendance.

I know I'm going to get a lot of heat for this, but I didn't experience a ton of racism growing up. I am well aware that I am a white Anglo-Saxon Protestant, and WASPs predominated Lake Forest, so I know I was spared a lot of unnecessary, painful, hurtful nonsense. However, I attended progressive and liberal learning institutions, and I'm not saying racism was nonexistent; it just wasn't tolerated. My friends were white, black, Jewish, Catholic, Muslim, Asian, and Latin, and it really didn't matter to me. This was Chicago, and this was the 1980s. Our king was Michael Jordan, and our queen was Oprah Winfrey. Period. My mother adored Oprah, and she never missed watching *The Oprah Show*. I mean never.

My mother never made cheerleading or graduated college. Therefore, it was a given, since birth, that I was fully expected to make cheerleading and graduate college. As much as I loved field hockey, I tried out for football cheerleading and made varsity as a sophomore. My mom was proud! I started out in all the top classes as usual. I was always in honors or some sort of advanced placement. I also really started to discover boys, and I was certifiably boy crazy. I started taking advanced acting classes and helped choreograph some dance moves for cheerleading. I played Ursula in a school production of *Bye Bye Birdie*. Kelly Perine played the lead, Conrad Birdie, and playing one of his fans was not a stretch. Kelly was so talented; it was an honor to share a stage with him. I developed a crush on him and ended up kissing him during driver's ed. Kelly went on to Los Angeles to be a huge success. He had a recurring role on *The Drew Carey Show* and a sleuth of other extremely impressive accomplishments.

My bust began to grow larger during my sophomore year. All those breast exercises I did while reading Judy Blume's *Are You There God? It's Me, Margaret* really paid off. (Wink.) I was rail thin with a C cup. The most comical part of these "new developments" was that older classmen students started saying "hello" to me in the halls. I was popular at the Academy as well. Many kids knew me from the day school, and the others seemed eager to be my friend. I just conquered the day-school crowd with ease; every crowd thereafter was a breeze for me. I personified rich, cool girl popularity. I had it down. As early as fifteen, I saw sex appeal as a valuable female commodity, and I milked it very well for years and years to come. I continued to sleep in my back brace, which developed my posture, but I was still relatively clueless about who I was and where I was going.

The summer of 1987, I got my driver's license and was granted a brand-new Audi from the Porsche/Audi Exchange in Highland Park. That was the summer the partying really started. Partying as a verb is fitting, because that is all I cared about and all I did. On my sixteenth birthday, I attended a keg party during the day in Lake Forest at a private residence next to the Winter Club and went to the Cure concert that night. Alcohol was always available at every social occasion. In a lot of homes, the parents were drinking right along with us. It was just the way it was. I lost my virginity to a friend who was home visiting from boarding school. It was nothing romantic or special. I mostly ran with different groups of people, and we all hooked up with one another. I ran with everyone: the preppies, the burnouts, the intellectuals, and so on. I hung out with and was liked by very cool people. I had a little crush on Vince Vaughn and kissed him a couple of times through the years. He was a year ahead of me at Lake Forest High and was extremely talented, funny, and magnetic, even as a young man. We were all like hamsters crawling all over one another. We called it "hooking up" and viewed it as no big deal. I had a few boyfriends here and there, but nothing special, and monogamy wasn't for me.

However, drinking was for me. It was like magic. It made me feel more confident, beautiful, funny, a better dancer—fill in the blank. In high school, I was a weekend warrior. I hit it hard every Friday and Saturday night. My grades slipped, and I crashed my Audi. This was remedied with a private tutor and a brand-new Ford Tempo, the only American car at the time that came standard with a built-in airbag. My mother viewed my partying as par for the course. I would go to dead shows and drop acid, and I started using cocaine with my drinking. I loved the fact that I could consume vodka like water while blowing lines. I still remember my first sunrise, staying up all night drinking and doing blow. My drug and alcohol use was purely recreational at this juncture. I was not physically or chemically addicted at this time. I wanted to go to a good college, so I buckled down and got really good grades the first semester of my senior year. This desire for a higher education coupled with my parents' money opened doors.

3

"To be beautiful means to be yourself. You don't need to be accepted by others. You need to accept yourself."

—Thich Nhat Hanh

When my brother was at the Academy, he had a best friend named Ted. Ted was a year younger than my brother and an impressive young man. Ted went on to Harvard and even received a Fulbright Scholarship to New Zealand. Our mothers became friends. When Ted was living in Boston, he met and fell in love with a lovely woman who attended Boston University (BU) and told my mother about BU's College of Basic Studies (CBS). Boston University hosts a variety of colleges. CBS was a two-year program that covered basic subjects, and after two years, students could go on to any other BU College. With this insight, I applied directly to CBS, got in, and went on to graduate from BU's College of Communication on the dean's list.

A lot of people ended up CBS students by default, meaning they applied to Boston University and ended up as a CBS student conditionally. I wouldn't have been one of those candidates; I partied a lot in high school, and I just didn't have the grades. I believe the only reason I got in was that I applied directly to CBS. The first day we were told to look to our left and our right. We were told that one of the people we were sitting next to would not be there next semester, and they were right. The college was graded on a bell curve, and you had to work hard if you wanted to stay. The two-year college offered an integrated liberal-arts core curriculum, taught through a collaborative team structure. CBS got a bad rap. The fact that the "B" stood for "basic" didn't help. CBS was called Charlie Brown School, Couldn't Bribe Silber (the former president of BU), and a whole litany of derogatory remarks. I found the comments quite funny, and I was just happy to be there. CBS hosted quite an impressive group, including Carolyn Bessette-Kennedy and, quite frankly, most of the popular crowd. CBS ultimately changed its name to CGS, College of General Studies. I presume someone feels "general" is much more impressive than "basic."

In the fall of 1989, my parents drove me to Boston for college. We had a fancy, tacky Chevy van that was very comfortable to ride in. It had a TV and a full bed and was stuffed to the gills with all of my designer clothes and Laura Ashley bedding. I was designated a roommate from Maine who never showed up. I was assigned a new dorm on Commonwealth Avenue with four other suite mates. Two were opera singers with very impressive voices. The other two girls were on some sort of academic scholarship. I was there because I was full tuition, and in 1989, Boston University was unequivocally the most expensive school in the country. It was more expensive than the Ivy League.

Boston University is a private research university that was founded in 1839. It has a total undergraduate enrollment of approximately eighteen thousand, and its urban campus sits on 135 acres in Boston, Massachusetts. Boston University ranked forty-second in the 2015 edition of *Best Colleges*. After visiting my brother at school in New Hampshire, I knew I wanted to go to school in a city, with more action. I found Hanover lovely and picturesque, but I wanted to go to a school that was on concrete, not in some field.

I still had my high school boyfriend when I started college. I understand how this can be a disadvantage. It's like bringing sand to the beach, but he lived in California, and the relationship was long distance. His name was Don Clark, and he had boarded at the Academy while I was a day student. We were best friends who fell in love; it was very *When Harry Met Sally*. Don was the captain of the football team, very good-looking, and hysterically funny. His grandfather coached USC football, and Don grew up tossing the football with O. J. Simpson and riding in helicopters with Al Davis. At the Academy, he was simply known as Surf; he was tan and athletic, and the nickname suited him.

I was Don's first love, and he wanted to move out East to be close to me. He was very loving and would cry at airports when he had to leave me. He called me constantly, and I loved all of the attention. When my parents first dropped me off in Boston, I didn't know anyone, so I flew to California to spend time with my boyfriend and drove down to Mexico to party. I got into the bars in Tijuana with my BU student ID. Apparently, I was in between fake IDs; I got a new fake one as soon as I got acclimated in Boston. I had gotten my first bogus ID at sixteen and used fake IDs consistently for underage drinking until I turned twenty-one.

Boston University had a Greek system, and I rushed first semester freshman year. Joining a sorority provides an excellent platform to gain experience and knowledge necessary to develop strong leadership skills, but I was just looking to meet boys and drink beer. My mother was an Alpha Phi in Wisconsin. Alpha Phi was top notch at BU, so rush for me was just going through the motions, no stress. This didn't stop me from wanting to dress to impress. Everything I wore to rush was Adrienne Vittadini from Neiman Marcus, and my shoes were typically Joan & David or Salvatore Ferragamo. They all loved me, and I kept getting extended bid after bid.

Alpha Phi International Women's Fraternity was founded at Syracuse University in 1872. The sisters knew I was a legacy and zeroed in on me during rush. It was a done deal. Greek life was great. I had new cool friends and a built-in social schedule in one of the best college towns in the world. My first week, we took a booze cruise in the Boston Harbor. I had a suitable ID in place by then. I just needed to maintain a 2.0 GPA to achieve initiation. This was the best dangling carrot ever. I was happy to study and maintain good grades if that meant I could stay and play.

Doreen, the sophomore who became my roommate, was an excellent student. She was just what the doctor ordered. I couldn't have wished for a better academic influence. She literally broke out in hives during final exams because she took them so seriously. My mother could not believe her good fortune with my roommate and offered up whatever she could to encourage our living situation. Doreen helped me get my ass in gear and take school seriously. I became an excellent student and was quite proud of my academic career. I am very grateful for Doreen and her positive influence. I ended up sharing a kickass townhouse with her and two other women my sophomore year.

Sophomore year, Surf started school at the University of Connecticut (UCONN), in Storrs. UCONN was founded in 1881, and visiting from Boston, I was less than impressed. Surf started on the football team, but he pledged Delta Chi and became a playboy partier and forgot all about football—and, eventually, all about me, too. I was fine with it; we were living separate lives. I was done driving to Storrs, because I got a parking ticket every fucking time. He was also kicking it (totally denied it at the time, but he admitted it and we laughed about it years later) with the chick who was in charge of handing out the parking violations for the dormitory lot. She had it out for me, and I knew it. In fact, I still find it funny.

In full disclosure, there was another reason I was deterred from returning to Storrs. One late night, after drinking into the early-morning hours at the Delta Chi house, I was arrested for DWI. Unfortunately, it was not uncommon for me to be drinking and driving at this phase in my life. When I got pulled over, I was drunk and belligerent. Apparently, I failed the field sobriety test because I didn't follow precise instructions. The physical sobriety tests entailing balance and agility, I passed with flying colors. Well over a decade in ballet lessons had served me well. However, the alphabet tripped me up. I was instructed to say the alphabet *K* to *W*. When I finished singing the alphabet song, the one I knew from *Sesame Street*, I went all the way to *Z*. This is when I was arrested for not following instructions literally to the letter. I told the officer I was just proving that I knew the entire alphabet; in this case, going the extra mile was not appreciated. I was an ignorant, entitled nineteen-year-old who admonished the police to be mindful not to scratch my Rolex as they were putting me in handcuffs. Shameful, but true.

I was so obnoxious they didn't even give me a Breathalyzer because they thought I was on drugs. I wasn't. In fact, I did some drugs sporadically in college and beyond, but alcohol was clearly my drug of choice. The bars closed in Boston religiously at two in the morning, and I was usually still up for more drinking, so I would either be drinking at a fraternity house or in Chinatown. If you went into Chinatown in Boston after hours and ordered cold tea, they would bring you a Miller Light. The only saving grace regarding my college drinking was that I typically took cabs. My grades were good, and it appeared that my life trajectory was positive, so any issues with my alcohol consumption were simply not acknowledged. I now know you can't change or improve anything that is not acknowledged.

When we arrived at the campus police station, I was in rare form. They wanted a urine sample and sent me into a tiny water closet with a sink, a toilet, and a female police officer. She ordered me to drop my jeans and pee in a cup. I started mouthing off. I accused her of being hot for me and stated that the only reason she wanted me to drop my pants was so she could get a better look. I was behaving inexcusably in retrospect, and I have no desire to sugarcoat my horrific behavior. I then had one of my "bright ideas." I decided that after I peed, I would dilute the urine sample with water while washing my hands. She witnessed this horrible plan and counted the sample as a refusal. At this point, my parents had a lawyer on the phone, who asked for additional testing:

breath, blood, or urine. The department recorded my foiled urinalysis as a refusal, and they refused to administer any additional tests.

As instructed by counsel, when I was released from the station, I drank cranberry juice, induced vomiting, and went to a hospital for an elective blood-alcohol test. I was still over the legal limit hours later, so this excursion was futile but worth a shot. I was found not guilty because my lawyer argued that the campus police were the ones refusing additional testing, not me. I was grateful for the verdict, but part of my punishment was that I had to attend alcohol-awareness classes in Hartford, Connecticut, on Monday nights for a few weeks. I had little remorse and found driving to these classes to be a pain in the ass. These classes also convinced me I didn't have an alcohol problem. We filled out a typical alcohol questionnaire, which asked questions about consumption and drinking alone. I admitted to having a beer in the shower while getting ready for a night out. No problem here. The class instructor admitted to losing his job as a result of his drinking. He showed up for work one Monday morning and was fired for being absent the entire previous workweek. He thought he had just been on a weekend bender. He didn't realize his weekend bender included two weekends, plus an additional workweek. This guy clearly had a problem, not me. I deemed myself alcohol-problem free, completed my class obligation, and compared myself out of there.

College continued to be really fun. My grades were stellar, and I was really popular. The country was in a recession, but my father was a big-time Chicago trader, selling premium, so my parents kept raking it in hand over fist. I volunteered for Bush/Quayle, and that was a fond time; I met a lot of cool people. Growing up in Lake Forest, being a Republican was pretty standard. Everything I knew was external; I was underdeveloped emotionally and didn't have a lot coming from within... yet. I still was very close with a lot of my Lake Forest friends and partied with them every time I was in Chicagoland for holidays or breaks.

During this time frame, I got three nose jobs and liposuction on my chin twice at Highland Park Hospital. I got these procedures done on the down low, and the results were so subtle that no one even noticed.

I clearly remember the looking-glass theory from my sociology class freshman year at CBS. I don't care what anyone says, Boston University's CBS gave me an enlightened, broad look at many subjects. In 1902, Charles Horton stated that a person's sense of self grows out of society's interpersonal interactions with and the perceptions of others. I am what I think you think I am. The term refers to people shaping their self-concepts based on their understanding of how others perceive them. This boils down to how we see ourselves, and it does not come from who we really are but rather how we believe others see us. This resonated with me because I placed a lot of value on other people's opinions of me. All of my self-worth came from external sources. My internal life was remarkably dormant. Being the daughter of wealthy parents, I could coast this way for a while. I remained well educated and well dressed. It's quite apparent and disturbing how far a Rolex and a Chanel bag could carry one in a recession. I had many convinced that I had it going on, and most importantly, I'd convinced myself. I could function as rich-kid dependent, but after graduation I fell apart at the seams. A runaway train…

4

"Your real influence is measured by your treatment of yourself."

—A. Bronson Alcott

My senior year of college, my parents joined Exmoor Country Club and bought a beautiful, grand house on Lake Geneva in Wisconsin. Exmoor is an exclusive country club in Highland Park, Illinois, founded in 1896.

The club's name was inspired by the English country setting of the popular nineteenth-century British novel *Lorna Doone: A Romance of Exmoor*. My parents had their own version of rush. My father had to be sponsored by ten members. Only men could join. My mother used to joke that you had to be a member with a member to be official. My parents' friends were instrumental in orchestrating their initiation. My mother wanted a suitable place for my wedding reception. I didn't even have a boyfriend. The new summer house was on Lake Geneva in Walworth, Wisconsin. It was a charming lakefront property with distinctive white pillars, a private pier, and a forty-three-foot-wide lakefront porch. The word "charming" is typically real-estate code for small, but this five-bedroom home was authentically charming and dazzling. The exact year it was built is listed as unknown, but rumor has it Ernest Hemingway summered there. Harry Carey had a summer home nearby, so it wasn't unusual to hear a small crowd sing "Take Me Out to the Ball Game" on any given summer night.

Easter weekend, my senior year of college, I started a nightmarish self-abuse cycle that went on for years and had devastating results. I turned into my own worst enemy overnight and couldn't get off the self-destructive merry-go-round. We had just returned to the Lake Geneva house after a delightful, yet filling brunch at the Abbey, a local resort and spa. My brother and his wife, Liz, were inquiring about my postgraduation plans. Liz was a graduate of Smith College, a private liberal-arts women's college in Northampton, Massachusetts, founded in 1871. The line of questioning was innocent and curious, but I had no answers. The next thing I knew, I was in an upstairs bathroom with a well-manicured finger down my throat, vomiting up my brunch.

I applied to law schools that clearly were out of my league. This was news to me. I was rejected by Pepperdine, UCLA, USC, University of Chicago, Northwestern, Boston College, and even BU. Ouch! The LSAT consisted of 50 percent logical reasoning, 25 percent reading comprehension, and 25 percent logic games. I scored a 141 (51st percentile), and it just wasn't good enough, even though I had straight As and was on the dean's list. I was also planning to move to Los Angeles with a sorority sister who ended up extending her stay in Florence, Italy, and changing her mind about the move. Instead, in April 1994, I moved to New York City with two different sorority sisters. This changing of roommates and coasts is telling of how uncertain I was about my future.

It felt like my life was spinning out of control, so developing an eating disorder gave me a false sense of control. I felt like I could control what I ate, what I didn't eat, the amount of food I kept in my body after a binge, the amount of time I exercised, and the all-important number on the fucking scale. The food noise provided an escape and a numbing of sorts. My disorder was secret and shameful, and I wasted so much time and energy self-harming with food. This wasn't uncommon for women my age. Growing up in the land of "you can never be too rich or too thin" didn't help. I knew a lot of female peers who were struggling with eating disorders, some more public than others. One girl from Lake Forest High School walked around with her hospital X-ray from when she swallowed her toothbrush. Sorry, no punch line. This kind of shit was commonplace. I kept mine superprivate, not even entertaining discussing it with a professional. I feel compelled to be transparent about this struggle at the risk of feeling mortified or embarrassed. My mother knew about it, but she turned a blind eye. I didn't share my disease with her, but she deduced the bulimia by the damage to many of our thirteen bathrooms. She mentioned the filthy bathrooms just once in passing, but Bertha was at our house two days a week, so the bathrooms never stayed that way too long.

In the fall of 1993, I moved back in with my parents in Lake Forest. I enrolled in acting classes at Northwestern's downtown campus. I was studying Chekhov's *The Seagull* in a building that was also designed by the same architect who designed my family's home, which I was living in…again. I felt like a loser, living at home after living on my own for years. This, coupled with an eating disorder, caused my self-esteem to keep plummeting lower and lower. I had no idea that my newfound self-pity was part of my egomania. I had a ton of friends in Chicago, so my social life was quite active. I would go through an entire Miss USA beauty regime, just to go grab a pint at a local pub. The worse I felt about myself, the more effort I put into the external.

In April of 1994, I moved to 600 Columbus Avenue, Eighty-Ninth and Columbus, NYC. I moved in with one sorority sister who was working for *Rolling Stone* and another who was an executive assistant, and I was going to pursue acting. It was a three-bedroom rental apartment, and my bedroom included a private bathroom—a must for a bulimic. I got new head shots. I was mass mailing and making calls. My first week in New York, I was an extra in a movie that shot at the famous Studio 54; my second week in town I was acting with dialogue on cable access. Some Kappa Sigmas from BU saw it and told me I wasn't bad. I knew I wasn't good, but I didn't know what to do about it. Acting, for me, was like barking up the wrong tree. I knew people from home who were extremely successful actors. They were also immeasurably talented and very driven. I was neither of these things and didn't have the balls to admit it. After looking at my résumé, one prominent casting agent told me to go home and marry a doctor. Going back to Chicago was not a viable option just yet because in my mind that equated failure.

I fell in love with New York City! I distinctly recall walking through Times Square, thinking I was in the center of the universe; and I believe that I was. My roommate worked for *Rolling Stone*'s Jann Wenner, so we were invited to some terrific parties. We all went to the opening night of the Broadway production of *Grease*. It was Rosie O'Donnell's Broadway debut. She gave a touching speech about her deep love of the theater and what New York theater meant to her in her childhood. During intermission, I was standing directly behind Donald Trump and Marla Maples. They were visually stunning! Say what you want about Mr. Trump—love him, hate him, indifferent—the guy is nothing short of impressive. I have been around immense wealth my entire life, and I was blown away! They looked like perfectly polished living art. This was New York, and New York is in a class all by itself.

While I was living in New York, I was completely subsidized by my parents, so I had a ton of opportunities and adventures, but it was bittersweet. I was getting work as an extra, which at first blush was exciting, but working as an extra is less than ideal. I was going out almost every night with my parental party fund. I knew a lot of people in New York whose company I preferred much more than my roommates'. Everything came to a head the weekend we were supposed to go to Woodstock '94. I ended up not going and eventually moved out. Our schedules were different because they had real jobs; additionally, I really wanted to live alone. I had lived alone my senior year and took to it like a fish to water.

I moved across the park to the Waterford Condominium, 300 East Ninety-Third Street, into a $1,300-a-month studio with great views of the boat traffic on the East River. I continued with extra roles in television and film, such as TV's *Law & Order* and the movie *City Hall*, which we filmed at the Brooklyn Academy of Music. I got to dance at the Tunnel one afternoon with Alec Baldwin and Anne Heche while filming extra work for the movie *The Juror*. While filming extra work, I never approached the stars. My false bravado wouldn't allow it. I was desperately trying to present myself as an equal, but no one was buying it, especially me.

I decided that I no longer wanted to be bulimic and switched solely to anorexia, with heavy white wine drinking and Marlboro Lights smoking, not to mention all the men. Brilliant! I'm glad I can laugh about it now. If not for my strong sense of humor, I would have put a bullet in my head years ago and been done with it. I have tried to apply humor to everything, and learning to laugh at myself has been therapeutic. When you learn to laugh at yourself, you never run out of material.

I got a job at Credit Suisse Group, playing an extra (bond trader) in the movie *The Associate*, starring Whoopi Goldberg. This was after I had decided I was done with binge eating, and I had a most unfortunate encounter with craft services, the film set caterers. I was disappointed with this setback, and so, in a proactive effort to avoid binge eating, I decided to attend an Overeaters Anonymous (OA) meeting in the East Village. Somehow I found this quaint, dark church basement. I walked in casually, noshing on a bag of garlic New York–style bagel chips. The whole place went fucking nuts, and it took me a minute to figure out why. Apparently, it's a big no-no to walk into an OA meeting with food. My faux pas. It's equivalent to walking into an Alcoholics Anonymous (AA) meeting with a drink. My bagel chip fiasco was frowned upon, but they allowed me to stay and attend the meeting. What happened next literally had me running for the door. Some of the people started introducing themselves as dual addicted, meaning food and alcohol. This annoyed the hell out of me. I wanted to talk about bingeing only. If sitting in an OA meeting meant that I had to examine my alcoholism even for a second, that was simply unacceptable, and I abruptly left. Again, I compared myself right out the door.

The good news was that I was no longer bulimic; the bad news was that I was on my way to becoming a full-blown alcoholic. The food noise was just part of my early twenties; it didn't last. However, the alcoholism had me by the short hairs and wasn't letting go. The reasoning that fueled my alcoholism is the work of a mental midget. Logical reasoning was half the LSAT, and I was exhibiting little to none in my twenties. I conceptualized that if I drank instead of ate, I wouldn't purge. I wouldn't want to waste the alcohol or the buzz. In my sick thinking, throwing up Chardonnay would be alcohol abuse. I successfully switched addictions, food for alcohol. What I didn't realize was that I was simply switching seats on the motherfucking *Titanic*.

I started losing weight and was really quite pleased with my appearance. My daily routine started with two to three hours of dance, followed by frozen yogurt at Tasti D-Lite, a place known for low-calorie products. I was given a lot of opportunity during this time frame and pissed all over it. I hooked up with Joe Franklin as "my manager." We talked every day for over two years. Joe was a NYC radio and television host personality. Franklin's show was first parodied by Billy Crystal on *Saturday Night Live*. Joe also appeared as himself in such New York–based films as *Ghostbusters, Broadway Danny Rose,* and *29th Street.*

One of the first jobs I got through Joe was an off-Broadway play. Just one "off." There were some off-off-off-Broadway plays, but this wasn't one of them. The play was *The O. J. Whodunit*, written by Larry Wolf Horowitz. I played Brandy, Kato Kailen's fictitious girlfriend. The satire play was a blast. It was a hot topic, and I would regularly see celebrities in the audience. Jackie Mason left during intermission. I was proud to be part of this production. We filmed footage for *Entertainment Tonight* at the Learning Annex. My mother got to see me on TV back home in Lake Forest, and that was a really big deal to her.

Joe had a reputation as a ladies' man and liked to be spotted with much-younger women. We were friends, and he never, ever came on to me, not once. He would come over to my studio for dinner. I would order him a steak dinner from Mumbles, because I didn't know how to cook yet. We would go to Rainbow and Stars at 30 Rock to watch Amanda McBroom perform. She is best known for writing "The Rose" for Bette Midler. I'm sure Larry told Joe about my party-girl shenanigans. For instance, I would tell Larry to meet me at Bella Luna for drinks, and I would have my best friend from Lake Forest, Liz, discreetly approach him at the bar and ask him if he would like to fuck. Larry would simply respond, "Where's Jane?"

Joe was an institution of New York City broadcasting. He was a living legend, and I was privileged to spend time with him. He would periodically ask me to come into his office to answer his phone. It was an old-fashioned telephone, the kind with the curly cord, and it rang nonstop. It was a trip to talk to so many different people. Joe truly loved people, and he took a genuine interest in them. He was always having me meet new people, and he told me that having curiosity was good for the soul. In my naïveté, I had no idea what he meant.

In typical New York, "Go See" form, Joe sent me to go meet Michael Bloomberg at his office, years before he was mayor. In the waiting area outside, it was like being inside a 7-Eleven with no cash register, no checkout. It was walls of refrigerators, fully stocked, and aisles of snacks—all complimentary. We had a nice meet and greet, and I helped myself to a granola bar on the way out. Joe sent me to meet Arthur Miller at his apartment a few times. I knew he was a writer but did not know to what degree. Arthur Miller was a playwright and a prominent figure in twentieth-century theater, and he was once married to Marilyn Monroe. I knew none of this at the time, which is probably why I got invited back. We shot the breeze and drank lemonade. He also had me meet one of the bigwigs of Ryder Trucks for dinner. It was never anything sexual or romantic. I was simply providing dinner company; and in exchange, I was getting schooled and enlightened. We would go to really exclusive dining clubs with no menus. When I asked for a menu, I was dismissed. These were the kinds of places where you would just express to the waiter anything you desired, and the kitchen would make it happen.

My drinking continued, and the New York *Zagat* was my social planner. I went out every night for dinner. I never had a shortage of friends; I actually had a waiting list to sit across the table from me while I guzzled Chardonnay and chain-smoked. I would always order an entrée and push it around my plate. If anyone commented regarding how little I ate, I would always deflect with humor. I would say something asinine like, "Jeffrey Dahmer told Pee-wee Herman not to play with his food, too."

I dated like crazy. I had men in constant rotation, but I wasn't sleeping around. I once went sixteen days with a different dinner date each night. I was shooting for an entire month, but I got tired. I couldn't let any one guy get too close, because they would see what a mess I was. I mostly dated investment bankers, making a couple hundred grand a year, but it never remotely impressed me. I would see my dad make their annual salaries in a week or even a day. I used to have a very skewed relationship with money. I remember one day in high school, my dad was down $350,000, and the next day he came home up $355,000. He happily reported to my mother, "Honey, we're up five grand for the week."

During this time frame, I let my guy friends get close—the ones I didn't fool around with at all. They really enjoyed me, too. I was up for anything and especially loved behaving in ways that guaranteed a ton of attention, like dancing on bars and going to strip clubs. I even got onstage at Scores New York. Scores had a wild notoriety and popularity. I was there one night, drinking Scotch on the rocks and smoking a cigar, when I decided I wanted to get onstage. I was wearing a typical LBD (little black dress), and I walked right up on the stage and starting dancing. The guys in the audience loved it, and two strippers got onstage and pulled my dress up to my waist. The crowd went wild, and one of the strippers yelled out, "She's wearing a thong!"

At this point, an announcer came on and said, "Good show. However, this is not how you get a job here, but we'd be more than happy to have you come in for an interview."

In 1996, I had my first panic attack, and I thought I was having a heart attack. A girlfriend from school, who worked for Morgan Stanley, sent me to her doctor. The office was really fancy. It was located in the Upper East Side between Park and Lexington. The doctor was well known in New York. Ten years later, I saw him on TV as magician David Blaine's attending physician for an underwater stunt. I described my symptoms, and they ran a battery of tests. He diagnosed me as healthy, but anxious. He asked me how I relaxed, and I told him wine helped; he told me to go home and pour a glass of wine. I followed his orders to the extreme.

The drinking started during the day—weekdays, too. This anxiety and shaking was the beginning of daily detox. It was all part of self-inflicted alcoholic torture that was becoming my life. I stopped pursuing acting because my drinking was crippling me. Joe was an extremely astute man who had seen a lot and was very knowledgeable of people and human behavior. One weekend he took me to a matinee showing of the play simply entitled *JACK*. It was a play about John Barrymore, a huge talent and a mess of a man. He struggled with alcohol abuse from the age of fourteen. The play showed the downward spiral of an alcoholic. I got the hint. He didn't need to draw me a picture.

Late spring of 1996, I received a phone call from my father. This was extremely unusual. My father never, ever called me. All communication was through my mother, with whom I was on the phone constantly. He informed me that the risk control rules of floor trading were changing, and he was worried about making money. This was his way of telling me that the New York gravy train was coming to an end. I couldn't continue the charade much longer, anyway. Acting wasn't working out, and I had no backup plan.

Alcoholics don't have relationships. We take hostages, and I was sick enough for my first one. Mike, the older brother of my friend Jeff, who was a Kappa Sigma at BU, lived a couple of floors above me, also at the Waterford. Mike, Jeff, and I hung out for years. They knew I was a train wreck but enjoyed my company regardless. I met Mike in Boston a couple of times. He was a graduate of Tufts University, established in 1852 and located in Medford, Massachusetts. He was very bright and very charming, with a superquick wit. We were friends for years before he became my boyfriend and primary caregiver. In typical alcoholic fashion, I was looking for a geographical change.

5

"Doing is never enough if you neglect Being."

—Eckhart Tolle

When things aren't going well somewhere, the less evolved conceptualize that a move will fix things. This rarely works because no matter where you go, there you are. I didn't know this yet. I even imagined that if I left New York and the whole struggling wannabe actress thing behind, maybe my relationship with alcohol would improve. No such luck. I wanted things to change drastically, so for my geographical change, I picked Singapore. Mike was game; I think I might have been in love with him, but I'm sure I needed him more. Needing somebody and loving somebody are two entirely different things.

Singapore, officially the Republic of Singapore, is a modern city-state island country in Southeast Asia. This move could not have been more poorly planned. We literally walked off the plane and had no place to go. Singapore was expensive, so we found a little hotel in Singapore's Little India for roughly US $100 a night. We stayed aimlessly for a few weeks and then decided to take the train to the beach in Phuket, Thailand. We fell asleep on the train and ended up in Bangkok. Bangkok is the capital and the most populous city of Thailand. Bangkok Metropolitan Region currently has over fourteen million people, dwarfing Thailand's other urban areas in terms of importance. The good news was that Mike was somewhat familiar with Bangkok, as he had previously visited the city with some of his fraternity brothers.

We took a cab to the Nana Plaza and checked in to the Nana Hotel. The Nana Plaza is the red-light district and rumored to be the largest sex complex in the world. The hotel was fair, and I had the best pad thai in the world. I couldn't believe the rampant prostitution. Every girl walked around saying, "You want sucky? Me number one best sucky." In 1996, it was reported that the average Thai farmer made around US $600 annually. It seemed like many were sending their children to Bangkok to prostitute themselves. You would see many traveling businessmen returning to their rooms with three or four girls at a time. The next day we were having lunch at TGI Fridays, and I ran out of smokes. The waitress sent me across the street to a bar where I could purchase cigarettes. It was really dark when I walked in, but just light enough to see young Thai men, sick and shaking under blankets. Their harsh reality was staring right at me, and it broke my heart.

We moved into the Hampton Inn. It had a great restaurant, a nice bar, and a pool. Living in Bangkok was fun and exciting, even though I still have no idea what we were doing there. We would walk out of the hotel and see an elephant standing in the middle of the street. Hundreds of motorbikes were constantly flying by, and people would typically ride them barefoot. I confessed to Mike that I was an alcoholic. It was like telling him the sky was blue. I said I wanted to quit. He called my mother and said, "Janie is an alcoholic."

My mother refuted, "She's on vacation. Let's leave this alone."

I went a full day without a drink, but I couldn't stay away from it. I just couldn't/wouldn't.

I ended up living back at my parents' house at the age of twenty-five. I felt like a failure, and I was an acute alcoholic. Mike went back to New York, and that was the end of that. I had a shit fit and explained to my mother that it was socially awkward for me to be living at home.

She concurred. What would people think? The first rule of life in my mother's house was that we don't talk about our problems. The second rule of life in my mother's house was that we don't talk about our problems. She cosigned a lease for me at 1330 N. Dearborn in Chicago. It was a spacious Gold Coast one-bedroom apartment with views of Lake Michigan for $800. She also cosigned a lease for a new BMW. My father was not happy about any of this. Her chronically overindulging me was a bone of contention in their marriage.

These new leases were conditional. I had to get a job to appease my father and get him off my mother's case. I agreed to work a whopping nine hours a week at Neiman Marcus in Northbrook, Illinois. I worked three nights a week from six to nine. I used the line from *Friends* that Rachel used regarding her employment at Bloomingdales. I joked that my working at Neiman's was like the mothership calling me home. I worked in fashion jewelry, and I became overly familiar with the likes of John Hardy, Steven Lagos, and David Yurman. I let my friends use my employee discount, so they would use my employee charge account; and in return, they would give me cash. This worked out great in the short term. As an active alcoholic, the thinking is really simplistic and short term. Alcoholism comes with a relentless mental obsession. The inner dialogue is like, "How am I feeling now? How about now? Do I need a drink? How about now? Do I need another drink? Perhaps a cigarette?" It is a relentless circus that you think will never stop. I always thought, *Why bother quitting drinking? I'll still be thinking about drinking constantly. I mean, fucking constantly, so why even bother?*

My father was struggling at work. A lot of floor trading became remote off-floor DOT trading, meaning direct order transfer. Technology was changing the world of trading, and a large percentage of floor traders were having difficulty with all the change. My father was part of this percentage. My mother was on her ear; not only did things *look* bad for our family, things *were* bad. My father was having a midlife crisis of sorts; my brother was already divorced, remarried, and having problems in marriage number two; and I was a drunk.

My mother has struggled with her weight my entire life. There were years when she joined the Diet Center, a really restricted regime, and lost weight and was feeling better about herself. But now her family that she put so much effort into was falling apart, and the stress of it was getting to her. I don't recall her ever having dreams for herself; all her stock was in us, and we were letting her down. The more weight she gained, the less willing she was to be seen in public.

She had an unreal home-shopping addiction. We had a room in our house adjacent to our bar and front door that was designed as a ladies' coatroom, with a half bathroom attached. This house was built for entertaining. The foyer and rooms were so large that we would get notes in our mailbox from producers and directors who wanted to shoot footage there. John Hughes wanted to shoot scenes for *Richie Rich* at our house. My mom shut that shit down. Not only was nobody coming in, but as her weight skyrocketed, she was becoming more and more agoraphobic. The ladies' coatroom had so much stuff packed in there, most of it in unopened boxes. If I was invited anywhere for a birthday or a shower, I would go into the ladies' coatroom, and my mom had all sorts of appropriate gifts. I would randomly grab a sterling-silver ice bucket or jewelry, throw it in a gift bag, and be good to go. My father confessed that she was charging over $10,000 a month to her home-shopping-network account.

My father was having a really hard time adjusting to remote off-floor trading. He left the floor and was renting out his seat. He was trading at an office in Northbrook through Bright Trading, LLC. Bright is one of the largest professional proprietary stock trading firms in the United States, with trading rooms all over the country. I started sitting next to him during trading hours for support and eventually started trading on my father's account. I was good. I was really, really good. I would watch the S&P graph so intently and trade accordingly. I would joke that a chimpanzee could do it, but that wasn't entirely true. It took discipline, and with trading, I had a tremendous amount of discipline. The number-one discipline was how to take a loss. Admitting a mistake and getting out quickly was essential for longevity in the business. I saw bustouts all the time. It's easy to be a winner, but how you handled a loser was what mattered. I used to joke that I didn't ride losers in my personal life, so why would I ride one at work?

I opened up my very own trading account at Bright's Chicago office off floor at the Options Exchange. My office and trading desk were on the seventeenth floor, and I opened the account with $25,000 gifted from my parents' money. It was a revolving door for ex-floor traders who couldn't adapt to trading's new world. I learned to trade off floor, so I didn't come in with old ideas. It was like playing Atari to me, except a little easier. I was remarkably good, and I was superfast. My main initial stock was CCI, which was Citibank before it merged with Travelers Group. I loved trading it. I was sitting at my desk, doing my thing, when someone came in to give me a message from New York's CCI specialist. The message was, "Tell that guy to lay off the Starbucks."

I replied, "Tell him I'm a girl, and I'm drinking Sprite." I was so fucking fast that I was annoying him.

Specialists are members of the New York Stock Exchange who display their bid and ask prices and are required to maintain a "fair and orderly market." This dried up for me when Citibank became Citigroup; apparently the Travelers' specialist took over at that time.

One day, in my first couple of months, I was trading Pfizer (PFE), and news came out that correlated male heart attacks with Viagra. The office manager screamed out, "Is anybody short Pfizer?" I was, but I didn't say a word. There were no bids, and I was short by pure luck. There were a lot of washed-up floor traders really struggling. Some would yell at me after bad days, stating that the only reason I was there was that my dad kept putting money in the account. It was mean and untrue. The ones who said this shit were on their way out, and I was just getting started. If I had a bad trade or a bad day, I would bitch and moan about it, but when I was raking it in, I was quiet as a mouse.

I was finally making my own money. Instead of feeling grateful or humbled by it, I felt quite the opposite. I felt entitled, and it was about time. I wanted to be a big noise with all the big boys, and I never had any business working in fucking retail. I was able to take full responsibility for my apartment and car leases. No problem. I was repeating in Chicago exactly what I had been doing in New York. I was out drinking at the best restaurants every night, except now it was on my dime, and I was "working." If I was up $2,000 (net) by eleven in the morning, I would go to the bars and start drinking. If I stayed out too late, I would come in and trade from one till three. I was trading my own money and had no one to answer to. I was living the dream, but money is a curse for the active alcoholic.

Chicago's trading community was full of misfits, and I fit right in. I use the word "misfits" because a lot of our personalities were the type that corporate America didn't want. I finally felt like I belonged somewhere—a feeling that I hadn't had since college—and it felt nice. This was the kind of crowd that wouldn't dare question a cocktail before noon. I cleared through First Options, and on the sixteenth floor, we had complimentary soda dispensers, doughnuts, and bagels. They used to also have complimentary beer, but someone shut that down after the crash of 1987.

I became a fixture at Ceres Café, located in the north lobby of the historic Chicago Board of Trade Building. It was rumored that Ceres poured more vodka than any other bar or restaurant in the country. One could see through his Bloody Mary. If anyone came in and ordered a double of anything, we would all just laugh and conclude they were from out of town. I spent thousands of hours of my life in Ceres but still managed to be well known at the surrounding bars, too. Alcoholics love to drink with other alcoholics. We don't feel judged, and we don't feel the need to curtail our consumption. With Ceres, I hit the mother lode; and even though I was sick, I was having fun.

6

"There is more to life than increasing its speed."

—Mahatma Gandhi

One night while out drinking wine with my girlfriends, I decided it was time to start looking for a husband. I decided on my trading desk partner, and the poor guy didn't have a fighting chance. I started taking an active interest in him the very next day and took him home that night. Within days, I had a boyfriend. The main thing I really liked about this guy was that I could talk shop with him. Trading was my favorite thing to talk about, and it was absent from my conversations with my girlfriends or other guys not in the industry. It's unrewarding to have a conversation about something when only one party understands the subject matter.

His name was Lance, and he treated me like gold when we first started dating. He would bring me roses once a week and made me feel valued. He was crazy about me and always gave into me. This gave him staying power. He was loyal and devoted from day one. He wouldn't even look at other women. It was nice to let someone in. My drinking problem was obvious, but in the beginning, he never gave me any crap about it. He was just happy to be with me, and I was ready to have someone, too. One morning in my kitchen, I was drinking an Amstel Light before work. I wanted him to catch me. Instead, he just called to me to hurry up, that our cab was waiting, and we had to leave right now in order to catch the eight thirty opening.

We were watching TV one night, and I put up my left hand, looked directly at it, and told him something was missing. He jumped right on it. When I was in college, I had seen a woman sitting at the bar inside Boston's Ritz-Carlton Hotel, wearing an emerald-cut diamond ring that I loved and knew I would copy one day. I had a replica made in Chicago's diamond district. It was a stunning emerald-cut, dazzling diamond set in thick white gold and just shy of three carats. I had him give it to me at Nick's Fishmarket while I guzzled champagne and dined on lobster thermidor. This was the peak of the relationship, and it was all downhill from here.

Trading continued to go well, but I needed a new desk partner. As a couple, we thought it would be prudent not to sit next to each other at work. The truth is, I didn't consult him or anyone else for trading advice. I just felt I didn't need it. I loved to talk trading in general, but I was cocky and wasn't looking to get or give any help. If someone asked me for guidance, I would say, "The best trading advice I can give is, if you have something that works, keep it to yourself."

I moved downstairs to the other Bright office on the fifteenth floor. The guys later told me that they weren't too thrilled about a lady coming into the trading room. What lady? In this environment, there were a lot of inappropriate conversations, blatant sexism, and a very strong theme of political incorrectness. People would answer the phones saying, "Not-So-Bright Trading." Again, I fit right in. None of this nonsense bothered me, especially if it was funny. For me, humor trumped all.

One day I brought in Girl Scout cookies, and a well-known former floor trader said, "The cookies are OK, but next time, please bring me some Girl Scouts." The guys later apologized to me, telling me that I was way cooler than any guy they could have hoped for. I knew this going in. As an alcoholic, with no sense of true self, I could be anything I needed to be—except sober.

The day-trading world was exploding, and everyone wanted in. People were taking their savings and opening up retail day-trading accounts. In 1999, a day trader went into two Atlanta trading offices and killed twelve people and injured thirteen more after losing over $100,000. Shortly after this event, it was mandated that we had to pass the Series 7 exam to continue trading. The Series 7 is commonly known as the exam stockbrokers take to get licensed. I found it superannoying that I had to take a stockbroker exam to continue what I had been doing successfully for two years, all because of some asshole in Atlanta. The exam required a 70 percent passing score. I was relieved to score a seventy-one; if anyone scored above 70 percent, the joke was that they studied too hard. The perfect score was seventy. This is a glimpse of the mentality I was surrounded by daily.

We booked Exmoor the summer of 2000 for my wedding to Lance. My mother and I went to the Vera Wang salon at Barneys and picked out a gorgeous gown. I modeled my flowers after the bouquets Charlotte's wedding party carried on *Sex and the City*. I had nine bridesmaids, and I chose the same Nicole Miller dress that Donna's bridesmaids wore on *Beverly Hills 90210*. The invitations were Crane & Co., and the menu was surf and turf. The rehearsal dinner was at Sullivan's Steakhouse, and my mother put the wedding party up at the Fairmont. Lance and I moved into One Superior Place, the new high-rise located on Superior Street, between Dearborn and State Street. It was a two-bedroom rental on the forty-fifth floor and, with parking, was over $3,000 a month. It had great views of the lake and an outside pool that had stunning views of the John Hancock building.

Our relationship was having problems and got really bad after the wedding invitations were mailed. We just stopped being nice and respectful to each other. I now know that you can't have a successful relationship without kindness and respect. I love the brilliant Dr. Maya Angelou quote: "When you know better, you do better." I was a selfish drunk who didn't know the first thing about relationships. It takes two, and if he started something with me, I'd fucking finish it. I was not one to take shit, and I used to love to argue; and I was good at it. Back then, arguing was just a stage to show off my mean sense of humor and my quick wit.

The morning of the wedding, I woke up in the Fairmont hungover from Sullivan's, followed by late-night drinks with friends, followed by splitting a bottle of merlot with my mother in my hotel room. I had someone from Elizabeth Arden coming to do my makeup. One of my bridesmaids sent me a bottle of champagne. I cracked that mother open and got the party started. Once I started drinking, it was on. I called downstairs and kept ordering more booze. I called friends and invited them over. By afternoon, I had a party going in full swing. I had my bridesmaids and some Kappa Sigma guy friends from college all come over, and my suite was rocking.

The ceremony was set in Lake Forest at the Lutheran Church on Waukegan Road, sometime early evening. I drank with my girlfriends in the limo the duration of the ride there. When I got to the church, I was drunk, which was expected; the problem was, I was drunk and dressed, but I didn't want to get married. I was chain-smoking in the back of the church, not wanting to walk down the aisle. My mother was not happy. She didn't really care for the guy and knew we weren't right for each other, but now was not the time. Her younger sister, Ginny, took charge and set me straight. Ginny was divorced and said, "Look, this is not a death sentence, and you can always get divorced. Everything is already paid for; now, get out there and get married." And I did. The truth is, backing out was not a viable option, not with my mother. The church was packed, the caterers were paid, and I was getting married.

The reception was fun, and people said it was a blast. The dining room overlooked the stunning golf course, the food was world class, the dance floor full, and the bar open. I was overserved, even getting red lipstick on my white Vera Wang gown. I am certain that I embarrassed my mother. We went to the Dominican Republic for our honeymoon, and I told him I wanted an annulment; he didn't know what that meant. I rest my case.

We ended up buying a new construction condo on the west side of town. It was OK; I can't denigrate it too much because I picked it. My mother was heartbroken I was living that far away from the lake. My drinking continued, and I kept going downhill. I would stay out late, drinking with the guys from the office, and didn't want to go home. One night I came home and got yelled at because he had dinner waiting for me. This really struck my mom's funny bone. Being from a different generation, she thought the inversion of stereotypical roles was highly comical.

The marriage was already a joke when Lance started laying into me about my drinking. In all fairness, the guy had a drunk wife whom he didn't get along with, so the marriage was mutually miserable. The master bathroom was mine, so I started hiding Bud Light tall boys under my vanity. I wasn't getting the kind of attention I wanted from home, so I had no problem getting it elsewhere and didn't even feel bad about it.

The trading world was continuously evolving, and I flew to Bright Trading headquarters in Las Vegas to learn about pair trading. The two founders of Bright met at a casino, counting cards. As a scalper, I cleaned up when the volatility and volume were high. I never kept anything overnight, and my livelihood depended on these conditions. Pair trading is a market-neutral trading strategy, which enables traders to profit from virtually any market conditions: up, down, or sideways. The strategy tracks the performances of two correlated securities, where the trader is typically long one and short the other. Examples of stocks that are correlated in this fashion are Merck (MRK) and Eli Lilly & Co. (LLY) or Walmart (WMT) and Target Corporations (TGT). The basic concept is that the trader can make money focusing on the spread of two stocks, regardless of market conditions. I found the seminar interesting, but not interesting enough to want to change strategies. However, I did meet someone.

I was an extremely high-volume trader. I traded between one hundred thousand and two hundred thousand shares a day, even if I only traded in the afternoon. I paid a penny a share, so if I paid $5,000 a week in commissions, that was a slow-volume week for me. One night after the seminar, a group of us met for dinner at Grand Lux Café inside the Venetian. As I was waiting for our party to arrive, I spied something that grabbed my attention and wouldn't let go. There was a guy with thick blond hair and bright green eyes, wearing a polo shirt with the Onwentsia Club Indian emblem. That was the Lake Forest club where I learned to ballroom dance in seventh grade.

I marched right up and stated, "You're from Lake Forest."

It was Vegas, in August, and I was wearing a tiny sundress. He lit up like a Christmas tree, and our chemistry was instant and undeniable. His name was Steve, and he explained that his brother worked as a golf pro there, and he had graduated from Lake Forest High in the mid-1990s. He was five years younger than me and was pair trading out of Bright's local office. We talked and laughed animatedly for hours. I loved the fact that not only did he look like he was from Lake Forest, he drank like it, too, matching me drink for drink. Impressive. I was having such a good time at one point that I sneaked into the lobby to call my mother and tell her about my new friend. She listened, but I could tell it was not the best news she heard all day.

We exchanged numbers and continued talking after I returned home. One morning I was talking to him on the landline before the market opened. Lance must have overheard, because after I hung up, Lance came in, picked up the phone, and hit redial.

When Steve answered, Lance said, "If you want to have an affair with my wife, why don't you fly to Chicago and get it over with?"

Steve was young and cocky and thanked him for the green light. The next few nights, I stayed at my parents' house, which wasn't unusual. I never liked coming home if I knew Lance was going to be there, and things between us were even more unsalvageable than usual.

7

"Pain isn't the truth; it's what you have to go through in order to find the truth."

—Deepak Chopra

On September 5, 2001, my father called me again, which was a once-in-a-blue-moon rarity. I saw the number on the caller ID and automatically assumed it was my mother, as we talked constantly. When I heard my father's voice on the other line, I intuitively knew something was very wrong. He asked me if I was sitting down and then said, "Mom died today."

This sent me into a tailspin panic, and I told him he shouldn't give that sort of news over the phone and asked him to drive downtown to see me. It was early afternoon, and I was not working that day for some reason, most likely because I had hit it too hard the night before. I needed a drink ASAP, but unfortunately the only thing alcoholic in my condo was me. Fuck. Three strippers rented the unit beneath us, and they were typically home in the middle of the day. I ran down the stairs and frantically banged on their door. I explained that I just learned of my mother's sudden death and begged them for a drink. One of them gave me a bottle of Corona, and I drank it as I paced back and forth on their wood floor. I expressed that I felt responsible for her untimely death because I was relentlessly bombarding her with all of my bullshit. They were really sweet and comforting. One of them handed me another Corona as soon as I slammed the first one, and they continued to listen attentively. We barely knew one another, but they saw me as someone who was in a world of hurt and treated me kindly and compassionately. I couldn't have asked for better neighbors or human beings for that moment. It made me feel like I lived in a world where human beings genuinely were concerned with and supported one another. This was a feeling I seldom experienced.

I made a conscious decision not to get loaded that night. I had very few drinks that night compared to my daily consumption. Why I thought this was a good decision is still a mystery. All I know for sure is that I felt life-shattering pain that night. I woke up periodically throughout the night, so heartsick that I thought I was going to die. My heart physically felt like a deep tunnel of hurt and loss. I wanted to vacate my own being. Again, the only thing alcoholic in my condo was me, so there was nothing immediate to grab for escapism. I couldn't take the pain and was dedicated to do whatever it took to avoid feeling like this again. I essentially stayed drunk for another eight years, with the exception of one graceful dry spell in 2006.

My father was behaving really inappropriately. I understand that people grieve differently, but within two weeks, he was sending women flowers, purchasing greeting cards with sexual references, and buying books on dating. What added insult to injury was that my mother's family was utterly convinced that my father killed my mother. They felt so strongly they even expressed their concerns to the Lake Forest Police Department. My parents had been having problems, and my father had quit trading around the same time I started. He spent his time putting a new roof on the Lake Geneva house and building new cement stairs to the beach on the bluff of the Lake Forest property. He went back to school and was studying to be a nurse. He kept saying that he didn't want to end up "real-estate poor," so he was prepping properties for sale. My mother's family thought the reason he was studying nursing was to find an undetectable way to poison her and then pour concrete over the evidence buried in one of the new beach steps. They still refer to him as "the murderer." My mother dropped dead from a heart attack on the kitchen floor. She was miserable and obese. Even though her death was sudden, with her awful physical condition, it was no huge shock. My mother's funeral was September 10, 2001. The next day the whole world was in grief, and very selfishly, I felt robbed of the significance of mine.

I was no longer welcomed in his home. When I was divorcing and losing my condo, he said the only help he would offer was that he was willing to drop me off at the Salvation Army. He moved in a woman we vaguely knew and was remarried within months. The condo was on the market, Lance moved out, and Steve moved in. Steve had lost his father as a five-year-old boy, and it was nice to be with someone who knew loss. He was constantly running out for my favorite Chardonnay and would drink with me out in the open all day long. I was accustomed to warm wine because I would get bitched at for having it in the fridge. Going from Lance to Steve felt like leaving jail for a vacation.

I went back to the diamond district and sold my ring for a little more than half of what Lance paid. This turned into the "let's forget my mom is dead and party nonstop" fund. Steve made me laugh and liked to play all day and was the perfect playmate for me at this time. I eventually stopped working and closed my trading account. I was not in the right frame of mind to be there, and I was smart enough to recognize it.

Divorce is hard. Lance and I were not in love, and we fundamentally didn't even like or appreciate each other; yet, divorce still left me with very strong feelings of failure and loss. Dealing with death and divorce simultaneously would be hard on just about anyone. Steve was a much-needed distraction for a sad, confused drunk. He drank more than me, which I initially thought was a perk, but it ultimately translated into "he was really fucked up, too." He started exhibiting signs of profound instability, and I had to let him go. Two healthy people work really well together. Two sick people can function together, too. A sick person and a healthy person do not match. And in my particular situation, two sickies did not make a wellie.

I moved out of the condo, leaving behind all the furniture. I threw my clothes in garbage bags and moved in with a man twenty years my senior. Retrospectively, this is textbook behavior for someone who feels like she was just orphaned. Simon was a friend and fellow trader who was a guest at my first wedding. He was brilliant, got a perfect SAT score, attended Harvard for a spell, and was a founding member of the Options Exchange. We legitimately liked and enjoyed each other's company. I used to meet him for lunch occasionally at Maggiano's throughout the years. Simon lived in a beautiful condo in Lake Point Tower. Lake Point Tower is the only Chicago skyscraper east of Lake Shore Drive. Lake Point Tower was one of the first all-electric residential high-rises in the world, and it beat the hell out of the Salvation Army.

8

"The results you achieve will be in direct proportion to the effort you apply."

—Denis Waitley

Simon had constituted an option arbitrage enterprise, in order to exploit, by electronic means, ongoing arbitrage opportunities between and among the several domestic American options exchanges. With the new century came the capacity to transmit transactions in listed securities options over the Internet to the markets and receive back reports of their executions in a timely manner. This was all happening in parallel with an SEC decision mandating that all options exchanges list all options classes. Prior to that time, there had been a tacit gentlemen's agreement between the leadership of the exchanges that each one would list the options of an assortment of issues comprising their own exclusive franchise. After all issues became multiply listed, each exchange generated real-time quotes for the markets, in other words, the bid and the ask of each option series.

At the time, there were perhaps three hundred thousand or more of such series. And very frequently—literally thousands of times per day—a situation would arise wherein the bid in one series on one or more of the exchanges would be greater than the offer(s) on one or more other exchange(s). A large proportion of these so-called "inversions" persisted for many seconds and even minutes. Therefore, with the aid of a piece of software custom designed and dubbed "TradeSpinner," Simon's traders had the ability to see "inversion" opportunities, as well as to immediately profit from them by dispatching orders to both buy and sell the same option, virtually simultaneously, thus locking in the difference in prices between the various exchanges, all of which were bound as autonomous marketplaces to make independent markets.

Simon was interesting and fun and quite smitten with me. He was much smarter than the local guys I was used to dating. He loved to go out to the best places in the city. If I was torn between the scallops and the whitefish, he would seriously suggest ordering both. Additionally, he knew what a drunk I was and didn't give me shit about it. He flipped the bills. Occasionally, he would make an offhand remark about the wine-to-food ratio on the bill.

He offered me a position of chief operating officer of my very own futures Introducing Broker (IB). An IB is a futures broker who has a direct relationship with a client but delegates the work of the floor operation and trade execution to another futures merchant. I had to pass my Series 3 exam for my new big-shot position. The National Futures Association (NFA) required an individual to successfully complete the Series 3 in order to become qualified to sell commodities futures contracts and options on commodities futures contacts. I passed my exam, was given my own office on the corner of LaSalle and VanBuren, and had some really impressive business cards printed. It was clear to everyone that I wasn't chosen for the position solely based on merit. I was the only one who thought I was somewhat deserving, but I did nothing with this opportunity and continued to drink all day at Ceres Café.

I married Simon at a Chicago courthouse, and the ceremony cost a whopping ten dollars. I wore a pale blue sweater (something blue) from Old Navy and a pair of jeans. I thought attaching myself to somebody older and successful would help me feel more secure with my place in the world, but it didn't. I always felt like something was off, and I had a longing for something more. I thought marriage to a well-known

Chicago businessman would fix me and help me feel safe. It didn't. The truth is, I never felt safe because I wasn't even safe from myself. I continued to abuse my body with an obscene amount of alcohol daily.

Alcoholism is progressive. I can say this with certainty because I've lived it. This is not something I concluded by reading it in a textbook. I kept going farther down the scale, but I didn't know how to stop. When I first moved in with Simon, I was still desperately trying to hold on to appearances. I moved in with him because I had no place else to go, and my drinking was too far gone to be gainfully employed. A lot of my friends stopped calling. I wasn't as popular after my mom died, because at the end of the night, I was invariably drunk and in tears. The inevitable crying made people scatter away from me like cockroaches when a light is turned on. I got invited to fewer parties and dinners with each passing pathetic, drunken year.

One night, my drinking landed me in Northwestern Hospital with a bunch of staples in my head. It was strongly suggested that I might entertain quitting, and I attended an AA meeting. The meeting was on North Avenue and referred to as the "mustard seed." They were talking about drugs, even though the meeting was an Alcoholics Anonymous meeting. I was convinced that these people didn't understand and ultimately couldn't help me. I received phone numbers, and I did call a woman on my list. I asked for guidance, and she told me to pray about it. I thought she was out there, but I tried it anyway. I prayed halfheartedly with one eye open on my wine stash. When I opened both eyes, my wine was still there, and I was off to the races. Pray about it? Ha! What would the next person on the list suggest? Rub a lamp? This all smelled to me like unadulterated horseshit.

There may be something a little cute about a tipsy young woman, but I was an acute alcoholic approaching my midthirties, and there was nothing remotely cute about it. Simon had a beautiful wine cabinet that

I kept drinking dry. I literally drank thousands of dollars of his wine. He had it mostly for show. It got to the point where I would have to go down to the convenience store in Lake Point Tower in the morning for two Budweiser tall boys just to feel "normal." The symptoms of the disease were unbearable. I would feel like I would die or stroke out when I ran out of booze. This daily detox routine took over my life. Alcohol was the master, and I was the slave, no doubt about it.

Simon purchased a condo for us on the corner of Schiller and State. It was a postwar, nondescript building with really low ceilings, and it needed work. This was not my first choice, but I went with the flow. The neighborhood was gorgeous and familiar. The apartment that my mom cosigned for me in my twenties was a block away. Simon and I weren't spending much time together anymore. Like many alcoholics, I was starting to isolate and now preferred to drink at home. His business was also starting to struggle for reasons I was not privy to.

I was thirty-four and started wanting a baby. I had very little self-care, yet I knew I wanted to be a mom, and I wanted to get pregnant. I bought an ovulation test and started planning accordingly. When my period didn't come, I went out and bought a pregnancy test. As I was waiting for my results, I knelt down on the bathroom floor mat and prayed in earnest. I was begging God for a baby. I was treating God like Santa Claus, desperately hoping for something I wanted. I had a fundamental belief in God, but I believed God didn't believe in me, because I felt like such a disappointment. I felt unworthy. This didn't stop me from trying to make a deal with God. In my desperate prayer, I told God that if he blessed me with a baby, I would do right by the child and be a good mom. The pregnancy test was positive.

I was thrilled and willing to change my alcohol consumption for the baby's sake. I could change my ways for my unborn child, who I thought was worth the effort. I was willing to care for this baby in ways I was unwilling to care for myself. I was too chemically dependent to quit drinking cold turkey. Many severe alcoholics die detoxing. I was able to wean off the booze by drinking beer. I justified the beer drinking by remembering that many young Irish children thrived off beer during the Irish potato famine. I was still sick and could justify any crazy concept in my own head.

My mom's younger sister, Ginny, really stepped up for me at this time. She knew I was an alcoholic in another failing marriage. Simon's business occupied two entire floors of traders at the corner of LaSalle and VanBuren, and the business was struggling. Traders were leaving, and office furniture was being moved home into our condo. She picked me up and moved me outside Philadelphia to live with her. We were all still sad about my mom, and it was a healthy environment for my pregnancy.

After I dried out, I needed to find gainful employment with health issuance before my belly started to show. At some point in time, Simon had canceled my insurance without telling me. I had already seen this movie. Lance did the same thing to me in my first marriage. Assholes. During my job search, I worked for my aunt's friend as a temp in Philadelphia's Historic District for fifteen dollars an hour. The neighborhood was gorgeous, and the antiquity was fascinating. It was rumored that the building I was working in was a residence once occupied by Alexander Hamilton. I would walk by Independence Hall daily and was starting to feel alive again. It was summertime of 2006, and downtown Philadelphia was beautiful; and I was actually feeling good. I wasn't drinking, I was gainfully employed, I had a supportive home life, and I was eating well. I was exhibiting healthy lifestyle choices for the sake of my unborn child—the same choices and behavioral changes I was unwilling to make for just me.

My résumé was impressive, with my education, experience, and professional licenses. I did not disclose my pregnancy while I was interviewing, and I didn't legally have to. My condition was protected under the HIPAA health insurance law signed by President Clinton in 1996. I ended up getting hired as a headhunter with excellent medical insurance. I was given my own office, and my job performance was mediocre at best. I didn't know the first thing about headhunting, and I was thrilled with my pregnancy. I received daily e-mails describing how my baby was developing inside my body. These e-mails helped keep me dry. I also read extensively about fetal alcohol syndrome online, and that also helped keep me from picking up a drink.

My daughter, Paige Elizabeth, was born at Thomas Jefferson University Hospital in Center City, Philadelphia, on December 29, 2006. My wish for a healthy baby was granted. I had a beautiful private suite in the maternity ward that I sneaked out of to go drinking my first night after giving birth. I found a diner that was attached to a crowded, smoky bar. I took a seat at the bar and, after a few rounds, started bullshitting with the other patrons. I simultaneously started smoking again, too. One guy I bummed a cigarette from asked me if I had any children. I proudly reported back that I recently had a daughter. He asked me how old my daughter was, and I showed him my hospital bracelet and told him she was roughly twenty hours old. He looked at me like I was nuts. I started to hear the crazy music again, and I knew my circus was back in town.

9

"Every human being is the author of his own health or disease."

—BUDDHA

When Paige was five weeks old, my father drove Paige and me back to Chicago. We arrived at the Gold Coast condo in the middle of the night. I was surprised that my key still worked, and Simon was home. I had not been in communication with him while I was living in Pennsylvania, but he was aware that I had given birth. He was thrilled to meet his daughter, and there was no drama. The typical boy-meets-girl love story just wasn't our story. We were roommates again, and we remained civil. He even set up a trading platform for me at the condo. He was offering me the ability to trade again, this time from home. I just wasn't comfortable throwing that kind of money around after working for hourly wages.

I was drinking again. Alcoholism is progressive, so I was right where I left off or even worse. Simon was losing his business, the marriage was long over, and the condo was up for sale. I was a nervous new mother who was starting to spin out of control again. Simon rented Paige and me a one-bedroom apartment at One Superior Place, the same building I used to live in with my first husband. Simon was never around, which was great. I had no idea where he was and didn't even care. I was drinking around the clock, again. My baby was on the bottle, and so was Mommy.

Simon rented a beach house in Ogden Dunes, Indiana. The rent for a house in Indiana was far less than the one-bedroom rental in Chicago. The house had beautiful views of Lake Michigan, and the next thing I knew, we lived in Northwest Indiana. I never, in my wildest dreams, ever envisioned living in Indiana, but as an alcoholic, you just go with the flow. It goes without saying that you are exchanging your power for drinking. As a drunk, I didn't have the wherewithal to establish and sustain my own residence, but that didn't stop me from trying. I posted my résumé online and wanted to go back to work. Meanwhile, I continued drinking and looking at the lake, which felt very familiar.

Even as a drunk, I got offered every job I applied for. I put Paige in day care and settled for a job in Merrillville, Indiana, but I had no business being there. I was used to drinking all day and just couldn't wait until five o'clock. I started going to TGI Fridays for lunch. Indiana had its liquid lunch crowd, too, but it paled in comparison to Chicago. Most mornings started with wine in my coffee mug while I did my makeup for work. With my new job came new boyfriends, and it was about time. My marriage had been over years ago, and it felt liberating to be out of the house. The problem remained that I couldn't control my drinking. My office manager knew I had a problem. You spot it, you got it. He was a recovering alcoholic with fifteen years sober, and he called me out after he stepped down from management. He was in AA, and I was sick and desperate enough to give AA another try.

I Mapquested the ten thirty AA meeting in Portage, Indiana. I walked into the little building that would eventually save my life. A pretty woman greeted me, and I apprised her that this was the first time in recent memory that I recalled making it to ten in the morning without a drink. Her brows lifted, and her eyes widened. She knew she had a live one. The real deal. I would later learn that you can find anything you are looking for in AA: drugs, sex, money, jobs, and friends; and if you're looking for a drinking buddy, you just hit the mother lode. However, if you would like to learn how to live a fulfilling life free of alcohol, that's there, too.

I was sick as a dog but still managed to maintain appearances. I was wearing a blue Oxford blouse with French cuffs and a preppy patchwork skirt. My hair and nails were done, and I actually bothered with tasteful makeup. They were not impressed. They knew I was a helpless drunk, and the mask was off, but I didn't trust them. No one was drinking, no one was sick, and no one was shaking. How could these people possibly relate to my daily alcoholic torture? These people couldn't possibly understand. I convinced myself that I was terminally unique and no one understood.

They gave me a typical first-step meeting that is standard for all newcomers. We are admonished to try to relate as opposed to compare. Many of us compare ourselves out the door. Again, I was no exception. My body was shutting down from alcoholism, but I still had my uninterrupted driver's license, and most of these people had had theirs revoked at some point. Maybe I wasn't really an alcoholic? That was a desperate falsehood that supported future drinking. To tell an alcoholic that he or she can never drink again is devastating. Our lives can be wretched, and we can be living in incomprehensible demoralization, but we still cling to the illusion that someday we will be able to drink socially. The last few years of my drinking career, I preferred to drink alone, and there was nothing remotely social about it.

When the meeting was over, I was shaking so badly I went and bought some beer. One of the old-timers recognized my condition and suggested whiskey. I was so physically dependent that I felt I had to keep feeding the beast. The good news was, this meeting was about alcoholism, and these people saw me. They saw my pain. I cried for most of the meeting. I had been so busy constantly trying to cover up my drinking for so many years, it felt good to tell the truth. Truth can be the best medicine. We are as sick as our secrets.

I wanted to stop hurting myself. As hard as it is to admit, a great deal of my pain was self-inflicted. If there was another human being who was responsible for the damages of my alcoholism, the blame game would be on. What if the person causing all the misery is you? It is one thing to walk away from an abusive relationship, but what if your abuser is you? This is tricky, but it can be overcome. In AA, the only requirement for membership is for a desire to stop drinking. I didn't even meet this requirement. I didn't want to stop drinking entirely. When they initially told me that the good news was that I never had to drink again, I did not take this as "good news." In fact, I thought it was horrible news. I thought they could teach me to drink normally, socially, without consequences. This is utterly impossible for me, but I didn't know it yet.

A smart man learns from his mistakes, and a wise man can learn from other people's mistakes, too. I was unable to put the plug in the jug long enough to learn anything from anyone. I continued drinking, and my consequences kept building. Alcoholics move at the speed of pain. My dad took my daughter down to his winter house on Boca Grande, a small residential community on Gasparilla Island, in southwest Florida. I missed her like crazy, but she was in better hands. It is hard for a mother to admit that she is unfit and her child is better off in other hands, but I knew it. I was there. I effectively became homeless, living with different friends; some I knew from AA, and some I knew from the bars. If someone said "hello" to me, I had trouble discerning if I knew that person from the bars or from AA meetings. I would drink myself into oblivion at night just to awaken to fear and pain the next day. The Four Horsemen—terror, bewilderment, frustration, and despair—greeted me every day when I opened my eyes. I was a shell of a person. I was unemployable, again. I felt like I wasn't even living; I was barely existing at best.

I was stuck, sick, hopeless, and helpless. The truth is, I have never seen anyone walk into an AA meeting on a winning streak. We show up because we are broken and bankrupt, physically, mentally, and spiritually spent. For me, AA was the last stop in town; and as much as I didn't like it, I knew it. My welcome everywhere else had been worn out. I had bartenders cutting me off, and I kept drinking. We come in sick and tired of being sick and tired. This still isn't enough. We have to be sufficiently sick and tired of being sick and tired to be willing to do something about it.

10

"Will you look back on your life and say, 'I wish I had, or I'm glad I did'?"

—Zig Zagler

The ego can be a strong drug. My colossal ego helped save my life.

September 14, 2009, was my last drink. I had just finished detoxing myself in the garage of the house I was living in. I had spent the past four days nursing Jim Beam and warm Bud Light Lime in the garage that belonged to some of Simon's friends. Isn't drinking glamorous? I sipped on a glass of merlot (my only drink that day) "for my nerves." I was just completing day five of detox for the umpteenth time and went to an eight o'clock AA meeting. I clearly recall two people (a husband and a wife), whom I found disreputable, ridiculing me for still drinking. Sidebar: they are no longer married, and both returned to drinking. They told me that it was OK if I never quit; most people don't. My mother always said to consider the source; and in this case, I had enough brain cells working to do just that. My ego decided this nonsense was unacceptable, and I haven't had a drink since. I now had the willingness that I was previously lacking. After the meeting, I went out with my new sponsor to study the big book of Alcoholics Anonymous.

It is commonly stated in AA that we don't have enough room for the people who need or even want this program. AA works for the people who want it, need it, and are willing to work for it. Wanting something and needing something isn't enough. One has to be willing to do the work. I was told don't drink, go to meetings, and you will be fine. This is dangerous advice, because our solution lies in our book, and we really need to spend time in that book with a sponsor to receive the help we need. This is the mandatory work that most people aren't willing to do.

A decision without action is just a decision. If nothing changes, nothing changes. AA meetings have become watered down, and without working the steps according to our book with a well-versed sponsor, our chances are less than average. I could not, would not, quit drinking just by going to meetings. I wasn't getting well through osmosis. I could hang around other recovering alcoholics, but their work and their recoveries would not rub off on me. It wasn't enough.

Alcoholism is a progressive disease, which brings me to two things I know for sure: (1) if alcohol is causing you problems and you continue to drink, it will cause you more problems; and (2) sobriety is progressive, too. If you are willing to do the work and are able to quit drinking, your life will get so much better. These keys to freedom and happiness aren't in anyone else's pocket. They are in yours, and you just need to be taught how to use them.

My bottom was when I was done digging. Step Zero: I am done. I am not willing to give up one more thing for my alcoholism. Alcoholism is the great remover. It will first remove everything that you care about before it destroys you and goes in for the kill. It is cunning, baffling, and powerful. I used to say that I lost everything due to my alcoholism, and that is not true. I gave away everything for my disease. The truth is, I put alcohol first. My alcoholism was all-encompassing and dictated my daily life for years.

I continued going to AA meetings. I could not quit drinking on my own, but we could as a group. My mother taught me that there was nothing I couldn't do, that I could do anything I put my mind to. This is great advice, unless you are an alcoholic. I tried stopping drinking, but I could never stay stopped on my own. I needed the support of the group. The chronic detoxing was brutal. My shakes would be so bad that my convulsing body would wake me up at night. The disease convinced me that I was drinking to live. I could not fix my sick thinking with my own sick thinking.

AA is full of clichés and catchy slogans. They kept telling me, "Keep coming back," and it actually sounded sincere. I still looked behind me to see if what they were saying wasn't meant for somebody else. I was told by countless members, "We will love you until you learn to love yourself."

Initially, I had no clue what they meant by this and would quietly think, "Keep your pants on, Romeo." The truth is, I didn't know that I didn't love myself. I used to say I would give my life for my only child. They pointed out that I was putting alcohol before my daughter, so where was I on this wacky totem pole?

It turns out our solution is spiritual and not logical. Our big book, the AA bible, is loosely based on the big, big book—the actual Bible. The program teaches us how to first love ourselves and, ultimately, one another. The goal is a firm understanding of Compassion 101. If you study the religions independently, compassion is the common denominator. I would argue that it is nearly impossible to chronically practice compassion when you really don't love yourself. How are you going to care for the other guy when you don't really care for yourself? This is the biggest problem facing the world today. Most people don't really love themselves and don't even know how. The good news is, this can be taught and transmitted.

We can all start over. It is possible for every one of us to live a higher life—one with self-love, self-esteem, self-respect, dignity, integrity, and compassion. It all starts with self-love, but we can't begin to fix anything that goes unacknowledged; and most of us are unaware that we don't love ourselves. How could we possibly conceptualize that we lack self-love when we are so selfish and self-obsessed that we mistake it for love? With all of our selfies and self-seeking ways, how could we not have self-love? What a glaring disconnection of epidemic proportions! We could use a do-over, and a new beginning is available to anyone who wants one. New beginnings aren't just for alcoholics.

The very first step is being honest with yourself. The truth is, if you can't be honest with yourself, you can't be honest with anyone else. To thine own self be true. Acceptance of self and current circumstances, no matter how ghastly horrible they may be, is mandatory. We need to accept our situations and problems as is. We don't need to like or approve of them, but we need to accept them in order to change it. Anything less than authentic acceptance is a negation from reality. It's like drowning in quicksand. One's need to first accept oneself is immersed in the quicksand before one can figure a way out.

If acceptance is the answer to my problems, what is it and where can I find it? The following piece, by Vincent P. Collins, helped me develop an understanding.

ACCEPTANCE: THE WAY TO SERENITY AND PEACE OF MIND

Facing Life
Sooner or later, everyone arrives at a point where life seems to have become too big to cope with. Life is never really too much for us, but it can seem to be. When this happens, we have to get life back in focus. We have lost our perspective, but it can be regained.

You may have come to think of the world as unspeakably vast—the earth, twenty-five thousand miles around, and outer space, full of unknown worlds. But, practically, the world is limited to your house, your shop, and your town. Even if you fly to India or Paris or Hong Kong, your world is no bigger than the interior of the airplane, and no farther away than the nearest airport.

You may have come to regard the world as teeming with millions and millions of people. In reality, your world consists of a very small number of people—those you live with, those you work with, and those you're acquainted with.

And the awful, menacing future, that unending nightmare of shadowy days and years! Can't even bear to think about it. Well, quit thinking about it all. You live only a split second at a time; that's right this minute. You can think of only one thing at a time, do only one thing at a time; you actually live only one breath at a time. So stop living in a tomorrow that may never come, and start living one day at a time—today. Plan for tomorrow, but live only till bedtime tonight.

In short, that big bogeyman, Life, can be cut down to his real size. Life is only this place, this time, and these people right here and now. This you can handle—at least today.

"But my life is just one problem after another!" Of course it is—that's life. I don't know how it is with you, but it took me a long time to realize that at least some of these problems were of my own making. For instance, I thought that it was my duty to try to solve other people's problems, arbitrate their disputes, and show them how to live their lives. I was hurt when they rejected my unsolicited advice. I finally learned that you cannot help people unless they really need help, are willing to be helped, want you to help them, and ask you to help them. Even then, you can only help them to help themselves.

An old Arab, whose tent was pitched next to a company of whirling dervishes, was asked, "Don't they bother you?"

"No!"

"What do you do about them?"

"I let 'em whirl!"

I caused myself a lot of unnecessary grief by trying to be "unselfish," to think of everybody else first, myself last, and to try to please everybody. But you can't please everybody. You can knock yourself out by doing this and that and the other thing to please "your cousins and your sisters and your aunts," and you find out that they are not really affected one way or the other. "Please everybody, nobody's pleased; please yourself, and at least you're pleased!" Charity begins at home, and enlightened self-interest is a basic endowment of human nature. You can save yourself a lot of grief by admitting the futility of trying to please everybody, or of trying to please somebody who just can't be pleased.

A surprising number of people believe that other people can hurt their feelings. They won't believe you when you tell them that it just isn't so—that no one can hurt you unless you let them! If irresponsible or unreasonable criticism causes you unhappiness, that is at least partly your own fault. We all say, "I don't care what people say," but the tragic thing is that we do care, and pretending we don't makes things worse. What to do?

Practice turning a deaf ear to the person who irritates or upsets you; make up your mind that you are not going to let yourself pay any attention to what "he" or "she" says, and mean it. This you won't believe until you try it. If you refuse at least to try it, some suspicious and cynical soul (like me, for instance) might suspect that perhaps you've got so in the habit of having your feelings hurt that you'd be bored otherwise.

So much for unnecessary suffering.

How about real trouble, trouble that comes regardless of what we do, think, or say? That terrifying problem that has no apparent solution? Let's stop for a minute and see what a problem really is.

A problem is a set of circumstances that threatens your well-being. And what are "circumstances"? Circumstances are people and things. So "solving our problems" really means getting people and things the way we want them. Sometimes we can do it. More often we can't. What then?

There are several things we can do. We can look around to find somebody or something to blame. Or we can put ashes in our hair, wear shabby shoes with run-down heels, accentuate our wrinkles, and make the rounds with our friends chanting, "Poor, poor me!" We can succeed in making our family miserable. We can haunt doctors. We can waylay our pastor, beat our breast, and blame God: "What have I done to deserve this?"

Acceptance

These various "home remedies" —blaming everybody, self-pity, and the rest—have but one result: they make everybody, including ourselves, more miserable and add our difficulties without solving them. Shall we "curse God and die"? No.

Do what the politician does: "If you can't beat "em, join "em!" If you can't solve your problems, learn to live with them in spite of them.

"Oh sure, sure;. just like that! All very well to say 'learn to live with them,' but it's another thing to do it! Just how do you go about doing that?"

Very simple, my friend, so simple you wouldn't try it unless you were desperate. If you are desperate enough, you'll try anything. So try something that works—try acceptance!

Acceptance is the only real source of tranquility, serenity, and peace. It is also known as "Surrender," "Bowing to the Inevitable," "Joining "em." It can be acquired if you have an urgent desire to help yourself and you are willing to ask God to help you.

Luckily for us, the perfect formula for acceptance, simple and practical as a can opener, is ready at hand, waiting for us to use it as hundreds of thousands before have. Written by Reinhold Niebuhr, it is known far and wide as the Serenity Prayer. Here it is:

God grant me the serenity to accept the things I cannot
change; courage to change the things I can; and the wisdom to
know the difference.

11

"There is a principle which is a bar against all information, which is proof against all arguments, and which cannot fail to keep a man in everlasting ignorance—that principle is contempt prior to investigation."

—Michael St. George

The gift of desperation brought me back into the rooms of Alcoholics Anonymous. To my dismay, they were still talking about God. I even saw the word "God" on the walls and found it disconcerting. I was ready to talk about and tackle my alcohol problem, and I didn't want to be bombarded by a bunch of holy rollers. It's not that I didn't believe in God; I was convinced God didn't believe in me.

I admitted to my innermost self that I was an alcoholic, and I accepted it. Now what? I inquired how this all worked, and I was told that "HOW" is an acronym for honesty, open-mindedness, and willingness. I was finally being honest about my drinking, but the sobering reality was that I was dying. I was walking in and out of emergency rooms, getting Ativan drips for detoxing, only to return to drinking hours later. Between the time of my first AA meeting in Indiana and the time of my last drink, I split my face open on a glass coffee table and had to have plastic surgery. My smile, which I was so accustomed to getting compliments on, is now crooked. I was lucky that my facial muscles were only mildly affected. One doctor told me that my kidneys were shutting down, but I was more concerned about brain damage. I was worried about alcoholic dementia and "wet brain." I did not want to return to drinking. I no longer saw drinking as a solution; I saw it as a problem. This problem was nothing new; the goal used to be to stay just drunk enough not to care, but now I was finally willing to do something about it. When you live in the solution, the problem goes away.

Alcohol destroys three parts of the brain: (1) self-preservation and self-care, (2) rational thinking and logical reasoning, and (3) short-term memory. When I was first drying out, I could not believe what a mess I had made of my life. I was an unfit parent, and I was living in an altered state of denial. Being honest about my circumstances was not easy, and I felt like crap about myself. Alcohol annihilated any remaining shred of my self-esteem. I felt like I had to reach up to touch whale shit. I was broken; I was poor; I was confused; I was hurting; and I was really, really sick.

I was told I was not a bad person trying to get good; I was a sick person trying to get well. Alcoholism has its stigmas, especially for us mothers, and I felt terrible about the circumstances that I had created. I was using AA as a revolving door. I kept coming back because I was sick and I had no place else to go. Thank God AA does not shoot its wounded. I was a really good example of a bad example for over a year. Watching me not receive the message right away helped sober up a lot of other people. They watched as my alcoholism progressed and my life became more and more painful, yet they welcomed me back with open arms.

I wanted to live. I wanted to get better, and for this, alcoholic meetings alone weren't cutting it. When the student is ready, the teacher appears. I asked the smartest man in the room to be my sponsor. Michael is a kind, tolerant, patient, and brilliant man. He told me I had every right to drink myself to death, but he also said that if I didn't want to do that, he would do whatever he could to help me. He knows the big book of AA better than anyone I've ever met. Michael is openly gay and worked at one of the steel mills for over thirty years. For the most part, men stick with men and women stick with women when it comes to sponsorship, but we were a good fit. Michael didn't care what other people thought. He wore nail polish to the steel mill and learned to ignore other people's negativity and nasty comments. I really admired this about him, and I knew he had a lot to teach me.

He knew I was worried about brain damage, and he first attacked my alcoholism medically. He explained that it wasn't that I didn't care about myself, but because the alcohol was damaging my brain, I was incapable of self-love and self-care. He also explained that alcoholism is a twofold problem: a mental obsession coupled with a physical allergy. I had a mind that was obsessed with alcohol and a body that was allergic, meaning that when I drink, I have a phenomenon of craving, leaving my body always screaming for more. There is no control over the amount. I needed to recover from a hopeless state of mind and body.

He told me that the solution for alcohol was spiritual. I had two choices: (1) keep drinking myself to death to the bitter end, or (2) accept spiritual help. There was no door number three. Faced with this fatal nature, I became as open-minded and as willing as only the dying can be.

I hid out in AA because I didn't trust myself. I went to at least two meetings a day, sometimes three. Additionally, I was meeting my sponsor, reading the book, and working steps. I was in an uphill battle; the sad reality is, most of us don't make it. Most women who drank like me are dead, and I didn't want to be another statistic. I had to change if I wanted to live.

12

> "Something amazing happens when we surrender and just love. We melt into another world, a realm of power already within us."
>
> —MARIANNE WILLIAMSON

Left to my own devices, I am self-destructive. It was suggested that I find a power greater than myself. No human power could have relieved my alcoholism. Lack of power was my dilemma. I was not an atheist or an agnostic, and it was up to me to find a God of my understanding. The word "God" was no longer scary; it was clear that he was my only hope. Hope for an alcoholic is a really big deal. AA gave me hope because I saw other members living rewarding lives free from alcohol. If there was hope for them, then maybe, just maybe, there was hope for me, too. AA offered me hope, and the power of hope saved my life.

I was told to choose my own conception of God. I chose a loving, all-inclusive God who is available to all. The God in the AA literature is a supportive God who is available to anyone with just a mustard seed of faith. I knew I was powerless over alcohol, so the God concept worked. My friend and sponsor, Michael, told me that he was raised with a punishing God who he thought would roast him in hell. This old concept of God, the one featured on the TV show *Maude*—"God'll get you for that, Walter"—just didn't work for me. He opted for a loving concept of God, which was very clearly working in his life. I really liked this idea. My God loves me and wants good things for me. He has my back.

I could not learn to love myself by myself. The power of human love had failed me time and time again. God and the good people of AA loved me back to life. I knew God was speaking to me through other people, and I was hanging on every word. I wanted to get better, not just physically but also emotionally. Just like there are different levels of alcoholism, there are different levels of recovery. I was a low-bottom drunk. As spirituality is the only known, proven treatment for alcoholism, I wanted and needed a ton of it. I didn't want to just be dry; I wanted to be happy, joyous, and free. I didn't want stale bologna recovery; I wanted bone-in ribeye recovery, Oscar-style, preferably from Morton's. The difference between physical sobriety and emotional sobriety is the difference between chicken shit and chicken salad.

Lying about my drinking was instinctive. I felt I had to protect the disease. It felt good to tell the truth. I wasn't drinking, so lying was unnecessary. This honesty was refreshing. When I said that I had two, three, or four months sober, it was true, and it was irrelevant what other people thought. With my history, it was difficult for some people to believe that I wasn't drinking, but I knew it was true. What I thought about me and my life trumped external sources. This was a deep shift in my thinking, and the first of many psychic changes.

When you quit drinking, the good news is that your feelings come back; the bad news is that your feelings come back. I felt like one throbbing, walking, talking, gigantic exposed nerve. I was learning to feel again. I almost drank myself to death over my precious little feelings. I was surprised that I didn't drop dead from the vulnerability I was experiencing now. It wasn't easy, but not only was I not drinking, I wasn't thinking about drinking. It's really easy not to drink when you're not thinking about it. The mental obsession was gone. I don't know precisely how or why it left, and I don't even care about the details, but, as promised, it was long gone. The main feelings are mad, glad, sad, and afraid, and any other feeling is a variation of one of these. The biggest surprise of these was glad. As an active alcoholic for most of my adult life, I didn't experience a lot of glad—not because good things didn't happen, but because when they did, I numbed the feeling. We called it "celebrating."

I was poor, and I was fine with it. I knew I had to work on me, and I'd have plenty of time to think about money later. The strangest thing about being poor for me was when someone would suggest doing something that cost money. For instance, I had a cracked windshield, and countless people would say, "You need to get that fixed." I didn't have the money to run out and get it fixed, but I didn't have the heart to volunteer this information. I am now very mindful of other people and their situations. I try not to say things like "You need to get this" or "You need to go there." The reality is, not everyone has the money.

I moved in with a friend of mine from AA, and his name was Buck. I had lived with Buck before I quit drinking, and I used to get loaded with his sister, who was my new drinking buddy. Hanging around AA, I was bound to find one. I cut my lip while drinking one night and bled all over the place. The next day he told me I needed to move out because he saw me as a liability and thought I was going to die in his house. Now that I was sober, I was invited to live in his house again. Members of Alcoholics Anonymous really believe in second chances.

For recovering alcoholics, it's our behavior that is watched and measured. We've taught people that our word is just lip service and no good, especially when it comes to our drinking. They are so sick of hearing "I'm so sorry" and "This will never happen again." It's like a guy playing baseball in the backyard. His ball breaks a neighbor's window, and he apologizes and pays for it. The next day he breaks another window and apologizes and pays for it yet again. Here's a thought: how about not playing baseball in the backyard? Changing the behavior precludes all the trouble it brings. It's annoying when a newcomer gets a thirty-day coin and goes out and "celebrates." It was just as annoying for people to watch me be in and out if AA for over a year. Some people called me "Welcome-Back Jane." It leaves people with the impression that AA doesn't work. AA works for the people who are willing to work it, but most return to drinking.

Having Michael as my sponsor was like hitting the jackpot. He's spiritually very mature. He's been meditating and studying spirituality for decades. He's gone in and held his inner child that was completely and blatantly ignored by an alcoholic father. Some really cool stuff! Like any good alcoholic, I wanted more, ever since the first time I meditated with him. Michael is very funny, and some of his humor is off-color. He loves to help people. He is well aware of his role. He knows that God uses him and requests to be used as a vessel. He says, "God, please use me. Use me like an old whore." God takes him up on it, and Michael feels honored. Michael is best friends with his God. It is a beautiful relationship. I was blessed to have him as a mentor, and I knew it. I was starting to value and appreciate other people. Wow!

13

"Nonviolent action, born of the awareness of suffering and nurtured by love, is the most effective way to confront adversity."

—Thich Nhat Hanh

My beautiful daughter, Paige, came to live with me at Buck's house. She was three years old and had no recollection of seeing me drunk, and I was hell-bent on keeping it that way. She started going to AA meetings with me when she was just a baby in diapers, and our reconnection was a superpositive AA story. I was so happy to be in her presence that that was all I wanted to do. I barely worked, and she didn't go to day care for over six months. We were living rent-free. Buck was a long-haul trucker, and we took care of his little white dog, Snowball, while he was on the road. Buck was the one who told me I needed whiskey at my first meeting because I was shaking so badly. He is a good man, and like Michael, he truly enjoys helping other people. I loved my new AA community. People like Simon and my dad would joke that I turned into Blanche from Tennessee Williams's *A Streetcar Named Desire*, depending "on the kindness of strangers."

This time I had with my daughter was one of my biggest blessings. We would go to the park; I would pull her around the neighborhood in a wagon, and she finally had the mother she deserved. It is a child's birthright to be loved, and I was finally able to love her the way she deserved. People say we have to quit drinking for ourselves, but if it wasn't for my beautiful, blameless child, I just don't know if I could have crawled out of the rabbit hole. I can't say I quit drinking for me. If it weren't for Paige, there is a good chance I would have died in my disease. Due to my drinking, the sad reality was that I wasn't even an active participant in my own life, so I was utterly incapable of being truly present. Paige was so sweet and loving toward me. It took a lot of internal work to not feel so undeserving of her love. It was still new for me to actually allow myself to feel love from another human being, even my only child.

Almost immediately after I quit drinking, I started running daily. Depression can't hit a moving target. Regular exercise offers emotional and physiological benefits that lead to a new sense of well-being. I don't know which was in worse shape, my body or my mind. The mental and physical damage continued to snowball downhill while I was drinking. I continued to go to AA meetings, purposefully seeking out the ones that I found had the most spirituality. I had to arrest my pattern of self-inflicted misery. My brain was really fried from all the drinking. During my first few months sober, I didn't know whether to shit or wind my watch. They told me to "bring the body, and the mind will eventually follow." It was a pleasure to get physically fit. It is nothing short of a privilege to care for myself today. It is superimportant for us mothers to take care of ourselves. Our children watch our attitudes and behaviors toward ourselves and mimic what they see.

When I first started attending AA meetings, I was told that I had a thinking problem, not a drinking problem, and this really pissed me off. I would think, *This isn't dollar therapy; this is about my drinking and a relentless, insidious disease.* I came to find out that drinking was just a symptom. We become what we think. I used to have a self-defeating mind. A concrete example of this was that I thought I could never quit drinking, and with that mind-set, I was 100 percent correct. When I believed God could relieve me of my alcoholism, he did. You will never go beyond what you believe. The way I feel about myself really matters; the way I talk about myself really matters; and the way I care for myself really matters. What I think of myself determines my place and my happiness in the universe. Our own negative thinking can create the biggest limitations on our lives. It is crucial to be kind to ourselves if we wish to be kind to others and have a positive influence on our fellow man. The very first step of compassion is learning to be genuinely kind to yourself. We can't transmit something to others if we don't have it for ourselves first.

As an overly sensitive alcoholic, I was very tuned in to the way other people spoke to me. Their words were in direct correlation to how I felt about myself on any given day. Yet, I paid little to no attention to the way I spoke to myself. I now recall that a lot of it was negative. "You're a drunk. You're a loser, and everybody knows it. Everybody thinks you are a screw-up, and they are right. You will never quit drinking. You don't deserve to be a mother to your baby. She deserves better than you. You're a piece of shit. Nobody fucking loves you. You will never be able to dig yourself out of this hole you dug." The negative self-talk went on and on. I knew that if I wanted to live a happy life, this needed to be corrected.

I needed to pay superclose attention to the way I spoke to myself if I wanted a life filled with self-love. Mirror therapy was suggested, and I was so desperate to change that I would have tried just about anything. Louise Hay's mirror therapy was instrumental in my learning how to love myself. I would look in the mirror, give myself a hug, look deep into my eyes, and say, "I love you. I really, really love you." It felt really awkward at first. This was one of those "fake it until you make it" exercises for me. There are even instructional videos on YouTube that you can readily access. I kept it up and continued to feel better and better. I was becoming comfortable in my own skin. I know many people who swear by it and give testimonials, swearing that the results are tried and true. It worked for me, and I still do it today.

Really cool results were happening. I could see God working in my life. I wasn't drinking, and I was being honest with myself and others.

I had radical hope; I had limitless faith, and I was able to be the mom Paige truly deserved. I reclaimed my integrity and dignity. I finally had some peace of mind. I was acquiring unbelievable gifts. These gifts they don't sell in stores, and if they did, I couldn't afford them. I'm proud to report that my self-talk has improved drastically. I now say things like, "Take it easy, beautiful. It's already OK, sweetheart. You look great. You're a really good person. That was a good idea. You're really smart." This transformation didn't happen overnight. It took me years and years of self-abuse to end up as helpless as I did. I didn't get better overnight, but the important thing is, I did get better!

Another thing I love to do now is to have God songs to listen to. I have always loved music and been a romantic sucker for love songs. I just didn't have any real love in my own life that I could relate to. Now that I have God's love, I am able to love myself and, ultimately, other people. I am nothing without God. He is the source of all the love I have in my life today. I now love to think of my God when I hear a good love song. My favorite God song of all time is Celine Dion's "Because You Loved Me." It makes me cry. One of Michael's God songs is "Take a Chance on Me." Either the ABBA or the Erasure version will do.

In the fall of 2011, Paige started preschool. I started working in earnest, and we moved into a quaint little rental in Miller Beach, Indiana. Miller is a community on the southernmost shore of Lake Michigan. Miller Beach is effectively Gary, Indiana. It is gorgeous with lush trees and a beautiful beach. I would see deer when I went running. Miller Beach is the closest beach/resort community to Chicago. It was also superaffordable. My job started going well, and I became successful as a national producer in my field. I finished sixth in the country in 2012 and 2013, and I finished fourth in the country in 2014.

I am so humbled by and grateful for all of the blessings in my life. A grateful alcoholic never drinks again. I am so grateful that people took the time to show me the way out of the woods. I was a hopeless, helpless drunk who learned to love herself. When you learn to love yourself, you are building something inside you that you cannot lose. Self-love has authentic power. It really is the greatest love of all. It is a love of unlimited potential. It feels almost as if I'm living on borrowed time. The reality is that I probably am. I thank God every morning when I first open my eyes. In God's economy, you don't need to deserve every blessing, but you must trust him and believe that his will is good. I am convinced that the kind of "second chance" that God gave me is available to anyone and everyone, not just alcoholics. We are all people who are flawed and made mistakes, but God loves us anyway; and if you go to God for help, he will help you. You have not, because you ask not. God is no descriptor of persons; then again, neither is alcoholism.

If you are struggling with the God concept, you can borrow my God. He already loves you and wants to help you. He wants you to seek him; all you have to do is ask. He is big enough to wrap his arms around all of you. He is available to anyone from anywhere, regardless of what you have done in your past. He wants to heal your life and take away your pain. He will do things for you that you can't do for yourself. This is a promise. The love of God is an open invitation, an open door, and an access point to positive love and energy—unlike the enemy or negativity that will just show up in your life, without even having the courtesy to knock.

I now know that the cause of my misery was lack of love. I lacked love from God because I shut him out. I lacked love and acceptance for self, others, and circumstances. No matter how much grace God offers, if you don't believe, you will never have it. Once I tapped into the love of God, my healing journey began. Acceptance coupled with spiritual growth is the answer to all of my problems. It's not always easy, but it is really simple; and like anything else, it becomes easier with practice, practice, practice. I have been granted the gift of a new state of consciousness and being. This gift is available to anyone who wants it, and I feel compelled to spread this message to all, not just alcoholics.

The better I felt about myself, the easier it was to feel better about other people. When I learned to love and accept myself and my circumstances, it was possible to practice love and tolerance of others. Alcoholics are some of the most selfish people on the planet. I learned I was not only selfish, but I was also delusional. I used to think I was only hurting myself, so let me be. I was hurting so much that it was difficult for me to see beyond my own pain. I was selfish, dishonest, self-seeking, and frightened, and these feelings fueled my drinking. When I sobered up, I realized I was the problem. I didn't just need to survive alcoholism. I needed to survive *me*. It wasn't my circumstances that were making me so miserable; it was my perception that was out of whack. When you learn to have love and tolerance of self, you naturally discover newfound love, tolerance, and patience for other people. I wanted to share my experience, strength, and hope with others. I know I have to give it away to keep it.

I spent so much time in isolation, desperately trying to keep myself disconnected from the rest of the world. I was not OK with myself, so it was challenging to feel OK with anyone else. Other people made me feel defective and inferior. I was living in fear. I was finally able to connect with others through pain and vulnerability. The more other people shared their pain and vulnerability, the easier it was for me to share mine. I was no longer alone with my pain. Pain was all I knew, so naturally, this was how I initially learned to connect to others. When people spoke honestly about their pain and devastation, it resonated with me. Their sincerity was palpable. I felt I could reach out and touch it.

14

> "When you judge another, you do not define them, you define yourself."
>
> —Wayne W. Dyer

People don't care what you know until they know that you care. The good people of AA showed me love and kindness. I didn't feel judged. This was such a relief. I judged myself without mercy for most of my life. I was unequivocally my own worst critic. The easier I was on myself, the easier I was on other people. I was developing empathy and compassion, and it felt good. I was well aware that I didn't learn to love myself by myself. I was learning new skills and concepts that were saving my life. Miraculously, I wanted to help others overcome their pain, too. I knew I would meet a lot of strangers in AA; I just never knew that I would be one of them.

As promised, my whole attitude and outlook on life had changed. It feels good to have the confidence to look the world in the eye today without guilt, shame, and remorse. I was shocked to learn that my horrific past, which I was so ashamed of, turned out to be my very best asset for helping others. Alcohol had beaten me into submission. I had to surrender to win. With abstinence came a healthier thought process. Logical reasoning was back. My battle with the bottle was a fixed fight. I learned that every time I stepped into the boxing ring with King Alcohol, I got my ass kicked, without exception. I was done wanting to kick my own ass. I was shown a better way to live, and I grabbed hold of it with both hands.

Pain led me to growth and change. Connecting with people on this painful level helped develop my sense of compassion. We were all people who tried unsuccessfully to escape pain, and now that we were connected, we were healing our pain collectively. I can't stay sober alone. I need the love and compassion of other human beings to live. I was letting go of my fear of getting hurt. I was starting to believe that what other people thought of me was none of my business. I also believe that if other people hurt my feelings, it is because I let them. I was like a barrel of apples, and I spent months taking out the bad ones (self-loathing, insecurity, and self-sabotage) and replacing them with good ones (self-love, integrity, and compassion). I was getting better, and I knew it. Any time an old tape ("you're no good") played in my head, I had the ability to correct it. It's not old behavior if you're still doing it. AA also stands for attitude adjustment. I can't live a positive life full of my potential with a bad attitude.

Compassion can come though pain and lead us to love. Other people noticed changes in me long before I noticed these changes in myself. I was told that it was rewarding for other people to watch me get better. When I was drinking, I was oblivious to my own behavior. I felt like I only had two brain cells left, and they were waving good-bye to each other. Another one of my new blessings was self-awareness. I was not only paying close attention to how I treated and talked to myself, but I was becoming mindful of the way I behaved toward others. Life took on new meaning. It is a real joy to watch other people recover. I have had the privilege of watching people transform their lives, and it brings me such joy. Compassion is beautiful, and it makes me feel good.

Meditation is another life-changing tool that the AA fellowship introduced me to. Some of the benefits of meditation are as follows: it helps you to manage stress, connect to your purpose, lower your blood pressure, attain laser focus, heighten intuition, improve memory, increase your immunity, decrease inflammation, boost your happiness, expand your awareness, decrease anxiety and depression, and cultivate compassion. Need I say more? My favorite benefit is that it enables you to become fully present, free from the pain of the past and the uncertainty of the future. If the word "meditation" puts you off, you can practice quiet time with deep breathing. This stillness will still serve you. You can also practice mindfulness, a form of meditation that can be done anywhere. Life itself becomes the meditation practice. Mindfulness equals awareness. It is a gift to be truly present. This is the direct opposite of taking your life for granted. When you take the time to be still, it positively affects all areas of your life, including the people around you, which can ultimately better the world.

Happiness is an inside job. Stop wasting time and money looking for happiness externally; it's not there. If you want physical health, go to the gym. If you want mental health, go within. The silence manifests intuition and guidance. I looked for peace of mind in thousands of empty bottles, to no avail. Peace is already within us, and practicing stillness or meditation is the best way to access it. Meditation has helped me intuitively handle situations that used to baffle me. It has given me a moral compass, a "God guide," if you will. It makes me want to be a good person and always try to do the next right thing. I don't worry like I used to. Worrying is also a form of meditation—a very negative one.

Sometimes we have to fall down to reprioritize what's important. Looking back at the pain, I see pivotal moments in my development. My faith was strengthened in the moments of uncertainty. When I felt uncertain, I learned to go to God, and he gave me strength and wisdom. Complete and utter failure started my movement into something greater. There is grace with every difficulty, so step into it. Those hard times were not happening to me; they were happening *for* me. Pain is a horrible part of the human experience, and no one is immune. After experiencing living in the pain funnel for years, I know pain. Pain led me from selfishness to compassion. It pains me to see the way people hurt themselves and one another. It is my theory that we first have to commit to self-love and self-care. Once we learn how to treat ourselves with respect and dignity, we can make the shift into treating one another better.

We are all the same. For some reason, we seem to ignore this commonality and focus strongly on what makes us different. Siblings even do this within their own nuclear families. It seems like when we look at one another, instead of focusing on the 99 percent we clearly have in common, we zero in on the less than 1 percent that is different. We use labels and distinctions that separate us. We need to stop distinguishing ourselves from one another. I hate hearing "those people" or "these people." If we were more loving toward and comfortable with ourselves, we would be more loving and tolerant of one another. This is a defeating exercise; we are all in this together, and we need to start acting like it.

I believe that we all come from love and return to love. Have you ever heard stories of an older sibling asking to be alone with a new baby who has just come home? When a parent inquires why, the child explains, "I'm starting to forget." I believe that we come from the Source of Love, and babies personify the purest form of love. I believe we are all here as spiritual beings having a human experience. In the grand scheme of things, I believe this human experiment is superbrief but filled with a ton of hurt and jam-packed with lessons. Pain is the pathway; peace and school are in session. I believe our faith is constantly tested. Intellectually, I know that the best way to pass any test is to stay at peace and trust God with every fiber of your being. This is a foolproof way to live life. It's easy to behave and trust God when things are going well, but our legacy is created in how we behave in the difficult times. How much we trust God and how well we treat others during the difficult times is what defines us. More important than our accomplishments are our character, our integrity, and how we treat people.

The main problem is letting our emotions get in the way and run the show, which is not wise. I let mine drive for years, and they drove me off the road. We must be determined not to stay angry at people or situations. If somebody unjustly wronged you, don't get mad—get better. Otherwise, it's like holding on to a hot potato and allowing it to keep burning your hands. Don't let anyone or anything take up too much space in your head rent-free. As humans, we experience so much negativity that we let way too much of that in, and it's horrible. Yes, utterly horrible things happen to good people every day, and there are some terrible people out there indeed! We just don't need to focus on the negativity. We create our own reality; so naturally, what we focus on magnifies in our lives.

I purposely try to avoid disrespectful, dishonest, and angry people. Negativity will cripple us if we let it. I've experienced a lot of joy and happiness, but it's hard to always live there. However, I pitched my camp in fear, year after year after year. Whatever you go through, love God and trust him to direct your life—G. O. D. (Good Orderly Direction). God can heal you everywhere that you hurt. You aren't hiding anything from God. He knows what is in your heart. He knows how much you trust him. God loves you and wants you to be happy. When you are happy, you are honoring God. Trade grumbling for gratitude and complaining for thankfulness. Be positive. Be happy. God wants us to be happy. We are here for only a small, finite amount of time. We should try to enjoy it to the best of our ability. Consider the alternatives: misery or death. Everybody has something to be happy about. Celebrate that you are alive today. God loves a party. Church is for people who don't want to go to hell; spirituality is for people who have been to hell on earth and don't want to go back. You can take on anything if your intentions are good and you approach it from a place of love and peace. Trust God, love yourself and others, and stay at peace...and you will take the world by the tail.

Everything you take for granted is a blessing. Everything you fear is a friend in disguise. Everything you want is part of you. Everything you hate, you hate about yourself. Everything you feel is the only Truth there is to know.

Everything you wish for is already on its way to you. Everything you think creates your life. Everything you seek, you will find. Everything you resist will stick around. Everything you let go of stays if it's supposed to. Everything you need is right where you are.

Every time you bless another, you bless yourself. Every time you blame another, you lose your power. Every time you think you can, you can. Every time you fall, you must get up and try again. Every time you cry, you're one tear closer to joy. Every time you ask for forgiveness, all you have to do is forgive yourself.

Everyone you see is your reflection. Everyone you know mirrors you. Everyone wants to be happy. Everyone wants to live in joy. Everyone seeks a higher purpose. Everyone breathes the same breath. Everyone needs love to survive. Everyone has a purpose to fulfill.

Everyone's the same as everyone else. We just get caught up in labels, names, skin color, and religion. Everyone's the same as everyone else. No one wants to feel the pain. Everyone's the same as everyone else. Everyone is dying for love to remain.

—JACKSON KIDDARD

Made in the USA
San Bernardino, CA
10 July 2017